Teaching
Speaking & Listening
in the Primary School

Also available

Writing Under Control (2nd edn)
Judith Graham and Alison Kelly
1-84312-017-8

Reading Under Control (2nd edn)
Judith Graham and Alison Kelly
1-85346-646-8

Language Knowledge for Primary Teachers (3rd edn)
Angela Wilson
1-84312-207-3

Teaching Literacy: Using Texts to Enhance Learning
David Wray
1-85346-717-0

The Literate Classroom (2nd edn)
Prue Goodwin
1-84312-318-5

The Articulate Classroom: Talking and Learning in the Primary School
Prue Goodwin
1-85346-703-0

Teaching
Speaking & Listening
in the Primary School

Third Edition

Elizabeth Grugeon, Lyn Dawes,
Carol Smith and Lorraine Hubbard

 David Fulton Publishers

David Fulton Publishers Ltd
The Chiswick Centre, 414 Chiswick High Road, London W4 5TF

www.fultonpublishers.co.uk

www.onestopeducation.co.uk

First published in Great Britain in 2000 by David Fulton Publishers
Second edition published 2003
This edition published 2005, reprinted 2005

10 9 8 7 6 5 4 3 2

Note: The right of the individual contributors to be identified as the authors of their work has
been asserted by them in accordance with the Copyright, Designs and Patents Act 1988.

David Fulton Publishers is a division of Granada Learning Limited, part of ITV plc.

British Library Cataloguing in Publication Data
A catalogue record for this book is available from the British Library.

ISBN 1 84312 255 3

Typeset by FiSH Books, London
Printed and bound in Great Britain

Contents

About the Authors

Lyn Dawes is currently teaching Year 5 at Middleton Combined School, Milton Keynes. She has published widely in the field of speaking and listening in the primary school and was previously involved with initial teacher education at De Montfort University, Bedford, and the Open University. She has also worked as Education Officer for the British Educational Communications and Technology Agency (BECTA).

Elizabeth Grugeon is Senior Lecturer in English in Primary Education at De Montfort University, Bedford. She has led a research team with Lyn Dawes, *Inside and Outside the Classroom: children's language development, 5–8*, and has a special interest in children's literature and children's oral culture. She is co-author (with Paul Gardner) of *The Art of Storytelling for Teachers and Pupils* (David Fulton Publishers).

Lorraine Hubbard was a primary school teacher in London and Devon. She was a researcher on the *Plymouth Early Years Language Project*. She is currently Senior Lecturer in English in Primary Education at De Montfort University, Bedford, with an interest in literacy in the European context.

Carol Smith has been a primary teacher and English coordinator for many years. She is currently a senior literacy consultant working for Milton Keynes Council. Carol is also a visiting lecturer to the University of Hertfordshire and De Montfort University, Bedford.

Sandra Birrell has recently completed a Primary BEd at De Montfort University, Bedford, specialising in English and D&T. This included five placements in schools in Bedfordshire. She was formerly a Registered General Nurse for ten years. She is now an NQT in a combined school in Bucks, teaching Year 1.

Acknowledgements

The authors would like to thank students and colleagues with whom they have worked at De Montfort University, Bedford, for providing examples of their own and children's work. In particular, they would like to thank the children, staff and parents of Portfields Middle School, Newport Pagnell, Milton Keynes. Also the staff and children at Southway and The Cherry Trees Nursery Schools in Bedford. The support, and the co-operation of teachers and children in schools in Bedfordshire, Buckinghamshire, Cambridgeshire, Milton Keynes, Northamptonshire and Norfolk, is gratefully acknowledged.

With thanks to Rosemary Smith, Lynda Gentle, Vyveanne Francis, Year 4 Primary BEd, De Montfort University, Bedford, for their contribution to the Epilogue; to Karen Martin and Sandra Birrell for their contribution to Chapter 2; and to the large number of De Montfort University students who contributed to Chapter 3.

In case of failure to obtain permission to include copyright material in this book the authors and publishers apologise and undertake to make good any omissions in subsequent printings.

Introduction

Elizabeth Grugeon

What is Speaking and Listening all about?

Talk is a wonderful ready-made resource that each child brings to the first day of school – unlike the resources for reading and writing that the school provides. The danger is that we take talk for granted; we don't think we have to do anything. This book aims to give talk a voice, to highlight it and give it the attention it deserves. For at the heart of literacy is oracy, and the way we access literacy is through oracy. Teachers and researchers are developing ways to assess speaking and listening, to find out how children are learning and to structure opportunities for language development. Recent government initiatives have had an impact on the way we understand and approach the teaching of speaking and listening. These will be constantly referred to throughout this book.

Curriculum Guidance for the Foundation Stage (Department for Education and Employment (DfEE)/Qualifications and Curriculum Authority (QCA) 2000: 44–5) puts the development and use of communication and language at the heart of young children's learning. The *National Literacy Strategy: Framework for Teaching* (DfEE 1998c: 3) puts speaking and listening at the centre of its definition of literacy:

> Literacy unites the important skills of reading and writing. It also involves speaking and listening which although they are not separately identified in the framework, are an essential part of it. Good oral work enhances pupils' understanding of language in both oral and written forms and of the way language can be used to communicate.

The National Literacy Strategy (NLS) framework and the introduction of the Literacy Hour have reinforced the importance of speaking and listening in the way the hour is delivered. The whole-class teaching component of the Literacy Hour requires a highly interactive, pacy oral exchange during which children need to pay close attention to the teacher and respond rapidly. Guided reading and writing sessions are also dependent on oral exchange between teacher and children while the independent group sessions require children to work in small, self-motivated, collaborative discussion groups. The document *Speaking, Listening, Learning* (QCA/Department for Education and Skills (DfES) 2003) has offered a critique of this type of oral exchange and seeks to encourage teachers to take the pacy exchange further in order to develop children's reflective and thinking skills by engaging in 'dialogic' talk.

The *National Curriculum* (DfEE/QCA 1999), in which Speaking and Listening represents a third of the Programmes of Study for English, has introduced both 'Group discussion and interaction' and 'Drama' under the heading 'Knowledge, Skills and Understanding', thus underpinning the more detailed prescription of the NLS. The four strands of speaking and listening (Speaking, Listening, Group discussion and interaction, and Drama) receive explicit and extended definition and support in *Speaking, Listening, Learning: working with children in Key Stages 1 and 2* (QCA/DfES 2003). For the first time, teaching objectives are covered in a systematic way; each strand is set out by year to show progression. Explicit links are also made between speaking and listening objectives and the objectives in the National Literacy Strategy *Framework for Teaching*. It is also a principle that objectives should be met in foundation subjects as well as in English and mathematics. The very detailed arrangement of the objectives is designed to ensure a systematic approach to planning teaching and learning within and between years.

This more explicit support for speaking and listening has put it on a par with the advice and support relating to the teaching of reading and writing. Speaking and Listening has tended to be an aspect of the English curriculum that is less rigorously and systematically planned, taught and assessed (Howe 1997: 1); it is an area in which many teachers feel that they need support and guidance. Teachers in training often feel this too.

Speaking and Listening in the classroom

To understand the position only a few years ago, consider the situation before the implementation of the NLS in 1998. A group of Primary Bachelor of Education (BEd) trainees were discussing Speaking and Listening in the National Curriculum. A latecomer arrived and the lecturer casually asked her, 'What do you think about Speaking and Listening?' 'I think it should come first in everything we do!' she replied. And the talk moved on to consider how we can make that possible. How we can create opportunities for talk that address the requirements of the Programmes of Study for English; how we can plan for Speaking and Listening across the curriculum. And how examples of good practice can be drawn from school experience. The students discussed their experiences in a range of schools.

In sharing their experiences it became evident that Speaking and Listening is hard to identify. Although it represents one-third of the statutory requirement for English, this does not always seem to be reflected in the amount of time that is spent on it, the amount of planning dedicated to it and the evidence of assessment taking place. One student observed that, 'Speaking and Listening seems to be limited to responses to questions and being quiet when the teacher is talking'. Another's impressions were very different: 'I am in a Reception class where Speaking and Listening is given a high profile'. This was achieved in many ways, 'in formal settings where children are expected to observe the pragmatics of turn-taking, answering only when asked to do so, in informal settings where children are observed speaking with each other and the teacher and other adults interact with the children'. In this classroom, Pauline observed children telling stories, being involved in sharing nursery and number rhymes, and all taking part in the Christmas production. She also noticed how children were being encouraged to talk about their activities and observed the teacher's careful way of giving all children a chance to talk and to develop their confidence as speakers.

Students in lower primary classrooms had seen many examples of this kind which they felt had provided useful models for their own planning and which had extended their understanding of Speaking and Listening: 'I've seen some really interesting teaching of Speaking and Listening when children listened attentively and asked sensible and sensitive questions'. This was on an occasion when visitors had come into the classroom during a project entitled 'Young and Old'. Students were also becoming aware of the cross-curricular nature of talk and of group work, and the importance of pupils being able to take control of their own learning: 'You can see how vitally important children's group discussions are, they appreciate the chance to be in control'. Others felt that their experience of Speaking and Listening had been fairly limited during their school experience and had not been aware of strategies being used either to promote or to assess Speaking and Listening: 'I have not seen any activity which a teacher has used to assess or develop these skills'.

This tendency was more pronounced for those students working with older primary classes: 'In my experience, Speaking and Listening has a very low status in teachers' planning. When I have tried to get children to discuss work in groups they have found this difficult. They don't see it as "sharing" ideas but as "copying". They feel more comfortable working individually so that the teacher gives each of them credit for their own thoughts'. Bernadine also wondered whether 'children have to be taught that although everybody has a different view, everybody's opinion is valid'. Caroline agreed that this was probably the case and raised another issue: that Speaking and Listening gives all children an opportunity to express their thoughts and opinions: 'I have witnessed discussion sessions in classrooms involving children confidently proposing ideas and opinions who would be unable to express themselves so well on paper'.

Several students were aware of potential problems, however. Di described how, 'during circle time, following a video or just during discussions in lessons, they are all very keen on speaking and getting over their ideas, experiences and viewpoints but not nearly so keen on listening to each other'. Again the seemingly low status of talk is mentioned. Kim observed that, 'apart from speaking as part of presentations, class assembly, Christmas performance, etc. all other speaking seems to be little regarded. Children are rarely encouraged to discuss with one another, to argue a case against one another or to justify. They are allowed a little pointless chatter, are required to answer questions when asked and occasionally have to explain why something is the case. Other than these uses, speaking is generally discouraged'.

This would be unlikely to be the case today since all teachers will be planning from the NLS framework and the *Speaking, Listening, Learning* objectives. However, at the time, others agreed that this was often their experience and as a consequence they felt less confident about planning for Speaking and Listening than they did for Reading and Writing: Anna admitted, 'I must confess that I am guilty of overlooking the importance of Speaking and Listening when planning my lessons and do not feel that I am a confident teacher of Speaking and Listening'. Many in this group felt like Anna. Kim raised other general concerns: 'Apart from being unsure about control issues, I would like to encourage more

Speaking and Listening and be able to teach such skills but I would be insecure about assessing these skills'.

Many students in training and newly qualified teachers may empathise with Kim in feeling that teaching Speaking and Listening could involve considerable risks. In the past, priorities in ITT have tended to squeeze the amount of time devoted to the subject. This is not likely to be the case in future; the English Orders (DfEE/QCA1999), the many NLS initiatives relating to Speaking and Listening during 2002, and the introduction of the new Key Stage 3 National Literacy Study Framework, where Speaking and Listening is a major strand, as well as the 2003 objectives, will all support a more confident approach by trainees and teachers. This book will provide a rationale for the centrality of Speaking and Listening in English and across the curriculum, based on evidence of good practice. It will provide an argument for developing talk in the classroom that gives Speaking and Listening equal status with Reading and Writing in the acquisition of literacy.

Speaking and Listening issues: a review

Teachers may well feel that everything in education has been undergoing major changes, not least as far as the teaching of English is concerned. The implementation of the NLS in 1998 was the focus of much attention; concern for standards of literacy will continue to affect children as they enter school, and new teachers as they enter the profession. In 2003 it became clear that English and mathematics could not continue to be the exclusive focus of efforts to raise primary standards. A more cross-curricular National Primary Strategy was introduced to replace the Literacy and Numeracy Strategies in order to help schools raise standards across the curriculum and to be more innovative and creative, taking ownership of the curriculum. The ideas behind the Strategy were set out in *Excellence and Enjoyment: A Strategy for Primary Schools* (DfES/QCA 2003, www.standards.dfes.gov.uk/primary). To encourage ownership by teachers LEAs would facilitate meetings and visits between schools so that effective strategies and initiatives could be disseminated. It seems that thinking had moved on since 1998 when *The National Literacy Strategy: Framework for Teaching* (DfEE 1998c) was introduced to raise standards in literacy. It was accompanied by a government target, 'By 2002 80% of 11 year olds should reach the standard expected for their age in English (i.e. Level 4) in the Key Stage 2 National Curriculum tests' (DfEE 1998b: 5). The new strategy was introduced in order to achieve this target, and it involved both the training of primary teachers and the professional development of serving primary teachers. For students in training the highest priority was to be given to ensuring that they were taught 'in accordance with nationally established criteria – how to teach literacy' (Literacy Task Force 1997: 22). The DfEE subsequently provided these criteria in *Requirements for Courses of Initial Teacher Training. Circular 4/98* (DfEE 1998a) followed by *Circular 4/98. Teaching: High Status, High Standards. Requirements for Courses of Initial Teacher Training* (DfEE 1998b) which has been revised and reissued by the Teacher Training Agency (TTA) in 2002 as *Qualifying to Teach: Professional Standards for Qualified Teacher Status and Requirements for Initial Teacher Training* (TTA 2002).

The ITT National Curriculum for primary English sent an 'unequivocal message about the importance of literacy by specifying the essential core of knowledge, understanding and skills which all primary trainees…must be taught' (DfEE 1998b: 20). *The National Literacy Strategy: Framework for Teaching* (DfEE 1998c) was accompanied by in-service education and training (INSET) for teachers in schools. Teachers, and teachers in training, have had to take on board a new focus on standards as far as their own knowledge and understanding are concerned (DfEE 1998a). Trainees have become accustomed to keeping a detailed record of their knowledge and understanding in relation to the standards required by Circular 02/02.

For children entering compulsory education a national framework for baseline assessment has become a statutory requirement. *Curriculum Guidance for the Foundation Stage* (DfEE/QCA 2000) describes 'stepping stones' towards the Early Learning Goals, which most children should achieve by the end of Reception, the foundation stage. The foundation stage curriculum is organised into six areas of learning, one of which is 'communication, language and literacy'. And here we find that, 'the development and use of communication and language is at the heart of young children's learning'. The revised National Curriculum for English (DfEE/QCA 1999) builds on this; the central importance of Speaking and Listening as the means of teaching and learning both Reading and Writing is reaffirmed. However, while the NLS does not make the teaching of Speaking and Listening explicit in the framework, it is implicit at all times. In the revised National Curriculum, the Programme of Study for Speaking and Listening at Key Stages 1 and 2 (DfEE/QCA 1999) extends 'skills' to include 'group discussion and interaction' and also 'drama activities'; under 'range of purposes' are specific suggestions as to what should be included such as, 'investigating, selecting, sorting, planning, predicting, exploring, explaining, reporting, evaluating' (DfEE/QCA 1999: 24). These skills underpin the requirements of the NLS and reinforce the centrality of Speaking and Listening.

Speaking, Listening, Learning and the Primary Strategy

The revised Programmes of Study for all National Curriculum subjects emphasise the importance of the interrelationship of Speaking and Listening, Reading and Writing in the provision of an integrated curriculum. The new orders stress these links: English contributes to the school curriculum by developing pupils' abilities to speak, listen, read and write for a wide range of purposes, using language to communicate ideas, views and feelings (DfEE/QCA 1999: 2). The government initiative, *Speaking, Listening, Learning,* as we have seen above (QCA/DfES 2003), has taken the aims of the Primary Strategy and explicitly links the speaking and listening objectives with those of the NLS and more widely with the foundation subjects. Speaking and Listening are now confidently seen in their cross-curricular context.

> The Primary Strategy is designed as a holistic, whole-school improvement initiative which will build on as well as incorporate, the former strategies for literacy and numeracy…this is supported by the new document Excellence and Enjoyment…which emphasises that creativity and enjoyment in learning are to be encouraged.
>
> (Harrison 2003: 5)

This commitment to creativity was broadly welcomed, as was the emphasis on schools taking more ownership of their own curriculum targets. The idea was to give schools more autonomy, 'to develop their distinctive character, to take ownership of the curriculum, to be creative and innovative and to use tests, targets and tables to help every child' (QCA/DfES 2003). The first publication related to the Primary Strategy was a new framework for speaking and listening. QCA's guidance *Teaching Speaking and Listening in Key Stages 1 and 2* (1999) was revised in the light of the NLS framework; a new package of materials, *Speaking, Listening, Learning: working with children in Key Stages 1 and 2*, appeared in schools at the end of 2003. This new material aimed to ensure that spoken language, including drama, would be specifically taught and that there would be explicit links between the literacy objectives in the NLS framework. More significantly, for the first time, there would be a specific rationale for progression in each of the four strands: Speaking, Listening, Group discussion and interaction, and Drama. And for the first time Speaking and Listening were a focus of the literacy strand of the new Primary Strategy. The new materials consist of two booklets containing an introduction and detailed termly teaching objectives and classroom activities that are often cross-curricular. Additionally, a set of posters suggests ideas for classroom planning and a video illustrates some of these. This pack is impressively detailed and prescriptive. There are over sixty teaching and learning objectives covering progression in the four strands from Years 1 to 6:

> There are four objectives suggested for teaching each term. Sometimes two are combined together where there is a particularly supportive link between them. In these instances, the two objectives are listed in the most logical order for the teaching sequence. In every term there is at least one explicit link made between a speaking and listening objective and one in the National Literacy Strategy Framework for Teaching.
>
> (QCA/DfES 2003: 5)

A more structured approach

The Handbook which accompanies the pack is deceptively slight but contains significant material outlining a far more structured approach to speaking and listening than we have seen hitherto; a far more detailed account of the relationship between Speaking and Listening and learning. A new concept, teaching through dialogue or dialogic talk, is introduced:

> Teaching through dialogue enables teachers and pupils to share and build on ideas in sustained talk. When teaching through dialogue, teachers encourage children to listen to each other, share ideas and consider alternatives; build on their own and others' ideas to develop coherent thinking; express their views fully and help each other to reach common understandings. Teaching through dialogue can take place when a teacher talks with an individual pupil, or two pupils are talking together, or when the whole class is joining in discussion.
>
> (QCA/DfES 2003: 35)

This concept is not unlike the 'exploratory' talk described in Chapter 6 and certainly the kind of talk advocated in the process of 'interthinking' (Mercer 2000). It has replaced the 'pacy, interactive' exchange of question and answer which was originally recommended in the Literacy Hour in 1998.

By 2002 (that is, five years after the NLS was introduced) there was a general feeling that children's competence in speaking and listening was being held back by the NLS:

> Research by academics has concluded that the literacy hour does not encourage the development of young children's speaking and listening skills to anything like the levels being arrived at in reading and writing. This is because verbal contributions of any significant length are severely restricted by the pressures of the hour.
>
> (Harrison 2002: 4)

Harrison refers to research published in the *Cambridge Journal of Education* (English *et al.* 2002) which showed that on average only 10 per cent of oral contributions by Key Stage 1 children in the Literacy Hour were longer than three words and only 5 per cent longer than five words. Similar research at London University Institute of Education in 2001 (Elmer and Riley 2001) showed that Key Stage 2 teachers were not asking sufficiently challenging questions and further research claimed that longer interactions between teachers and children had dramatically declined since the introduction of the Literacy Hour. Smith *et al.* (2004) carried out a substantial study which investigated the impact of the official endorsement of 'interactive whole-class teaching' on the interaction and discourse styles of primary teachers while teaching the National Literacy and Numeracy Strategies. The aim of this was to discover how far the intention to promote high quality dialogue and discussion had been achieved since the inception of the Literacy and Numeracy Hours. Their findings make depressing reading:

> Teachers spent the majority of their time either explaining or using highly structured question and answer sequences. Far from encouraging and extending pupil contributions to promote higher levels of interaction and cognitive engagement, most of the questions asked were of a low cognitive level designed to funnel pupils' response towards a required answer. Open questions made up 10% of the questioning exchanges and 15% of the sample did not ask any such questions…Only rarely were teachers' questions used to assist pupils to more complete or elaborate ideas. Most of the pupils' exchanges were very short, with answers lasting on average 5 seconds and were limited to three words or fewer…It was very rare for pupils to initiate the questioning.
>
> (Smith *et al.* 2004: 408)

Their data forces them to conclude that, '"top-down" curriculum initiatives like the NNS and NLS, while bringing about a scenario of change in curriculum design often leave deeper levels of pedagogy untouched' (Smith *et al.* 2004: 409). They suggest that there is a need for different approaches in order to change habitual classroom behaviours and that changing pedagogic practices is the major challenge to the future effectiveness of the strategies.

Bringing about change: dialogic talk – promoting extended talk and thinking

The effect that a lack of extended talk and opportunity to articulate ideas has on children's thinking skills has been recognised as a problem that needs to be tackled; it underlies the production of new materials intended to promote effective extended talk. The research carried out by Robin Alexander has had considerable impact on the Primary Strategy's recent publication *Speaking, Listening, Learning: working with children in Key Stages 1 and 2* and the accompanying video. This material has a new focus: the relationship between speaking and listening and children's learning. The original aim of 'interactive whole-class teaching', involving high quality dialogue and discussion, was described in the NLS framework as 'discursive, characterised by high quality oral work' and 'interactive, encouraging, expecting and extending pupils' contributions' (DfEE 1998c: 8). This has now been replaced by a new set of directives, under the heading 'dialogic talk', based on the research of Robin Alexander.

> Through his comparative research in the primary school classrooms of five countries (Alexander, 2000), Robin Alexander has shown that if we look beneath the superficial similarity of talk in classrooms the world over, we will find teachers organising the communicative process of teaching and learning in very different ways. …One of the reasons for this variation was that in some classrooms a teacher's questions (or other prompts) would elicit only brief responses from pupils, while in others they often generated much more extended and reflective talk. The concept of 'dialogic talk' emerged from these observations as a way of describing a particularly effective type of classroom interaction. 'Dialogic talk' is that in which both teachers and pupils make substantial and significant contributions and through which pupils' thinking on a given idea or theme is helped to move forward.
>
> (Mercer 2003: 74)

Implementing the confident use of dialogic talk in the classroom will require effective support for teachers and further research to provide evidence that interactive styles of teaching encourage significant gains in learning. This is beginning in 48 primary schools in North Yorkshire. Teachers are using video to analyse the quality of their classroom talk and in its second year significant developments are taking place (Alexander 2003): for example, teachers are giving children more thinking time and reducing pressure on them to provide instant responses; children and teachers are talking about talk and there is a shift in questioning strategies away from competitive 'hands up' bidding to the nominating of particular children whose individual capacities are taken into consideration (Alexander 2003: 65). Alexander feels that although the changes advocated challenge deeply rooted patterns of behaviour, they are achievable. The benefit for teachers and learners is children's deeper engagement with the learning contexts.

Changing patterns of behaviour: rethinking classroom talk

Responding to the guidance provided in *Speaking, Listening, Learning: working with children in Key Stages 1 and 2* (QCA/DfES 2003) will require teachers to consider making changes in the way they interact with children; many new and challenging ideas are introduced. A definition 'What is distinctive about speaking and listening?' (pp. 7–8) outlines the features of language that are distinctively oral and do not occur in a written form and which need to be explicitly addressed in the classroom. It emphasises the collaborative nature of meaning-making and the oral exploration of ideas. It stresses the importance of variation and range of spoken language and the need to teach children how to use this repertoire effectively. It suggests that children may explore the nuances of spoken language in drama and role play. A great deal of emphasis is placed on teacher talk, offering a list of 'dos' and 'don'ts' which reflect Alexander's research findings and recommendations.

Activity

You might like to look at the following list of 'dos' and 'don'ts' taken from the QCA materials, and consider which of the points characterise your own teaching. You might also like to consider where and when you have observed teachers or your colleagues using these strategies. How many of the 'do' column are familiar to you?

DO	DON'T
Choose questions and topics that are likely to challenge children cognitively	Merely ask children to guess what you are thinking or to recall simple and predictable facts
Expect children to provide extended answers which will interest others in the class	Tolerate limited short answers which are of little interest to other children
Give children time to formulate their ideas and views	Hope for high quality answers without offering preparation and thinking time
Provide models of the patterns of language and the subject vocabulary to be used	Expect children to formulate well thought out answers without the language to do so
Expect children to speak for all to hear	Routinely repeat or reformulate what children have said
Vary your responses to what children say; debate with children; tell and ask them things in order to extend the dialogue	Just ask questions
Signal whether you want children to offer to answer (hands up) or to prepare an answer in case you invite them to speak	Habitually use the competitive 'hands up' model of question and answer work
When children give wrong answers ask them to explain their thinking and then resolve misunderstandings	Praise every answer whether it is right or wrong

(QCA/DfES 2003: 22)

Comment

It may be that you felt that you recognised in your own teaching many of the 'don'ts' and were quite daunted by some of the 'dos'. You may feel that the 'dos' would slow the pace of your normal classroom interaction and that fewer children would be able to participate. You may be happy with the children bidding to speak by putting up their hands and would naturally respond to them by giving praise: 'good girl', 'brilliant', 'well done'. This is characteristic of the way teachers habitually behave in the UK; but Alexander is critical of the way we fail to give children sufficient thinking time or clear signals. He believes that 'the kinds of classroom talk which can be observed in many countries outside the UK ... provide some important pointers' to harnessing the power of talk to enhance children's learning: 'dialogue becomes not just a feature of learning but one of its most essential tools. ... we could profitably pay rather greater attention to children's answers to our questions and to what we can do with those answers' (Alexander 2004: 17–19).

Such critiques of the work of teachers are common among the educational research community. It is useful to remember that, despite such criticisms, teachers are responsible for helping to develop creative, purposeful people like yourselves! Alexander's undoubted breadth of vision can help us to see ways to refine and enhance our teaching. The change from 'interactive, pacy' NLS-style talk with children, to dialogic teaching, offers an opportunity to help children learn while becoming more articulate.

The main aim of this book, therefore, is to provide evidence of the value of Speaking and Listening and to support this by reference to classroom strategies that involve an integrated approach to literacy. There is a continuing need to demonstrate the centrality of Speaking and Listening to any definition of literacy.

Each chapter is self-contained, looking at different aspects of Speaking and Listening in the primary school. Chapter 1 provides an introduction to issues and the context for subsequent discussion, Chapter 2 looks at a range of practical concerns for early years' teachers. Chapter 3 combines practice and theory in looking at children's oral language inside and outside the classroom. Chapter 4 discusses the importance of talking about reading; it looks at small group talk in guided reading sessions. Chapter 5 discusses the way teachers achieve continuity and progression at Key Stage 2. Chapter 6 focuses on ICT work with older children, exploring the teaching of 'ground rules' for talk in small group collaborative activity. Chapter 7 looks at the implications of the Primary Strategy and *Speaking, Listening, Learning* for drama teaching in the primary school. Chapter 8 links issues for Key Stages 1 and 2 in an overview of different approaches to assessment.

Further reading

Alexander, R. J. (2004) *Towards Dialogic Teaching: Rethinking Classroom Talk*. Cambridge: Dialogos UK Ltd.

Mercer, N. (2003) 'The educational value of "dialogic talk" in whole-class dialogue', in QCA *New Perspectives on Spoken English in the Classroom: discussion papers*. London: QCA.

1

Speaking and Listening: An Overview

Elizabeth Grugeon

Prologue

As teachers we all have special moments of insight, 'epiphanies', when something we had never thought of or noticed before becomes crystal clear and nothing is ever the same again. Years ago, I was a part-time tutor on an Open University education course called *Language and Learning*. One of the assignments I had to mark was part of a study unit called *Language in the Classroom*, written by Douglas Barnes (1973). At the time, in 1973, this unit broke new ground by asking teachers to focus on the idea of 'classroom communication', of 'the classroom as a context for language' and of 'talking in order to learn'; these were new and challenging ideas for many teachers. Although teachers of English in both primary and secondary schools, at that time, were likely to feel comfortable about promoting interactive talk in the classroom, teachers in other curriculum areas tended to give small group collaborative talk a fairly low priority. Indeed, pupil talk was more likely to be in response to teacher questioning than initiated by the pupils; the amount of pupil talk in the classroom was very much related to issues of control and discipline.

The Open University assignment required the students taking this course – all of whom were practising teachers – to make a recording of a small group of children talking together as they undertook a particular task without a teacher being present. They had to transcribe the children's discussion and write an account of what seemed to be happening, looking for evidence of ways in which the children might be working together and helping each other to solve a problem or make sense of the situation they were dealing with.

This was a very novel idea at the time. Barnes had to give considerable encouragement to students doing the assignment:

> The longer you can spend working on the cassette tape and transcription the more you will understand about what is going on in it. It would be a mistake to dismiss speech as too obvious for close attention: the tape-recorder is making us aware of aspects of our behaviour which had previously hardly been guessed at. You will be making explicit to yourself perceptions which in everyday talk we experience intuitively, or perhaps not at all. Most of us have not learnt to be aware of how speech operates, so that learning to perceive what is going on in quite an ordinary dialogue demands care and patience.
>
> (1973: 21)

In asking his students to record children talking on their own, he writes:

> I want you to listen to a group of children talking when there is no teacher present to direct them. There are several reasons for beginning with children's uses of language when they are alone. Most importantly, it will allow you to see something of how children are able to adapt their language resources to cope with learning tasks.
>
> (1973: 20)

One of the students in my tutorial group was a teacher in a small rural primary school and her transcript and comments were to make a major contribution to my own understanding. We want you to read it for yourselves. Try to identify how the children are adapting their language resources to cope with the learning task, before you move on to the second part when the teacher comes into the room. The transcript is in two parts.

Transcript: Three children in a lower school, seven and six years old, discuss snails in a snailery, without their teacher present

Susan:	Yes, look at this one, it's come ever so far. This one's stopped for a little rest...
Jason:	It's going again!
Susan:	Mmmm...good!
Emma:	This one's...smoothing...slowly
Jason:	Look, they've bumped into each other (*laughter*)
Emma:	It's sort of like got four antlers
Susan:	Where?
Emma:	Look! I can see their eyes
Susan:	Well, they're not exactly eyes...they're a second load of feelers really...aren't they? No...and they grow bigger you know...and at first you couldn't hardly see the feelers and then they start to grow bigger, look...
Emma:	Look...look at this one he's really come...out...now
Jason:	It's got water on it when they move
Susan:	Yes, they make a trail, no...let him move and we see the trail afterwards...
Emma:	I think it's oil from the skin...
Jason:	Mmm...it's probably...moisture...See, he's making a little trail where he's been...they...walk...very...slowly
Susan:	Yes, Jason, this one's doing the same, that's why they say slow as a snail
Emma:	Ooh look, see if it can move the pot...
Jason:	Doesn't seem to
Susan:	Doesn't like it in the p...when it moves in the pot...look, get him out!
Jason:	Don't you dare pull its...shell off
Emma:	You'll pull its thing off...shell off...ooh it's horrible!
Jason:	Oh look...all this water!

At this point, the teacher came back and joined the discussion. It is worth considering what has been going on in this brief discussion before you read the second part. For example: how are the children interacting? How are they using language? Is there evidence of shared understanding?

Teacher:	Can you tell me how you think they move?
Emma:	Very slowly
Teacher:	Jason, you tell me, how are they moving?
Jason:	They're pushing theirselves along
Teacher:	How many feet can you see?
Susan:	Don't think they have got any feet, really
Teacher:	None at all?
Susan:	No
Emma:	I should say they've got … can't see 'em, no
Susan:	Haven't exactly got any feet
Emma:	Slide … the bottom … so it slides … they can go along
Teacher:	Doesn't it look like one big foot?
All:	Yes … yes (*murmur hesitantly*)
Teacher:	Where do you think its eyes are?
Emma:	On those little bits
Susan:	I can see … little
Teacher:	Which little bits?
Susan:	You see those little bits at the bottom
Teacher:	Yes? You think the top bits? Which ones do you think, Susan?
Susan:	I think the bottom one
Teacher:	You think the bottom … well, have a close look at the bottom horns, what is the snail doing with the bottom horns?
Susan:	He is feeling along the ground
Teacher:	He's feeling along, so what would you call the bottom horns, Jason?
Susan:	Arms? No … sort of …
Emma:	Legs?
Teacher:	You think they're legs, you think they're arms. What do you think they are, Jason, if he's feeling with them?
Jason:	Feelers?

Reflections on this episode

You may have noticed the way the children responded to this task; their thoughtful and creative use of language to explore and define what they were observing, 'it's smoothing slowly', 'It's sort of got four antlers'; the way they were working as a group, listening and responding to each other's contributions, 'I think it's oil', 'it's probably moisture'. When she listened to the recording, their teacher was surprised to discover what they were capable of observing and describing on their own and felt that she might have given them more chance to tell her what they had found out for themselves before she started on her own agenda. She was concerned by the way that she had asked closed questions that required a single word correct answer; an approach which did not encourage them to share speculations in the way they were doing when they were on their own. In Chapter 6 we look more closely at the way children work together in small discussion groups and consider whether this kind of 'cumulative' talk, where the speaker builds positively but uncritically on what the other has said, has its limitations. It is possible that when the teacher joins them they are beginning to need an adult presence; their investigative behaviour is beginning to alarm them, they are worried that they might harm the snails. The teacher, despite her misgivings, moves them on by helping them to use appropriate subject-specific language; Jason has learned the term 'feelers' by the end of the transcript.

It is a tribute to Douglas Barnes' pioneering work that we no longer find being asked to look closely at this sort of transcript surprising. At the time, my student and I were on a steep learning curve and I have never forgotten her amazement and the way she wrote movingly about the new insights that listening to her children working on their own had given her. She was surprised to discover what the children were capable of. She was delighted by the shared excitement and use of language to explore what was going on; describing, questioning, speculating, hypothesising and sharing ideas tentatively. She noted the way they used tag questions like, 'aren't they?' to include each other in the group, put forward their ideas tentatively, 'I think it's . . .' , 'it's probably', 'it's sort of . . .', 'well, they're not exactly . . .', 'it doesn't seem to . . .'; she noticed how they first observed and then tried to find words to explain what they could see, 'stopped', 'going', 'smoothing', 'bumped' and then focused on detail, drawing each other's attention, 'look', 'see', as they set up an experiment, 'let him move and we see the trail afterwards', 'see if it can move the pot'. Then, as she continued to analyse the recording, she described how when she returned to the classroom, her questions had put an end to this reflective talk, how by imposing her agenda she had given them no chance to tell her what they already knew and what was interesting them. She commented on the way in which she had taken over and finally produced the answers that she wanted without realising that they had already used the word 'feelers' on their own and talked about how the snails moved. She commented on the fact that out of 27 utterances, she had contributed 11, all questions, and that Jason had made only two contributions, both answers. When she transcribed the recording of what the children were saying before she joined them, she admitted to feeling mortified! And I shared this feeling, knowing how often I had imposed my own agenda on a class without listening to them and finding out what the children already knew. For me, this small episode marked the beginning of my participation in a growing awareness among teachers of the centrality of talk to learning and of the need to listen to our pupils and to ourselves as teachers.

Oracy: issues and concerns

You may be more familiar with the term 'literacy' than you are with 'oracy': it refers to Speaking and Listening and is spelt out in the Programmes of Study for English (DfEE/QCA 1999). At Key Stage 1: 'Pupils learn to speak clearly, thinking about the needs of their listeners. They work in small groups and as a class, joining in discussions and making relevant points. They also learn how to listen carefully to what other people are saying, so that they can remember the main points. They learn to use language in imaginative ways and express their ideas and feelings when working in role and in drama activities' (DfEE/QCA 1999: 16). And at Key Stage 2: 'Pupils learn how to speak in a range of contexts, adapting what they say and how they say it to the purpose and the audience. Taking varied roles in groups gives them opportunities to contribute to situations with different demands. They also learn to respond appropriately to others, thinking about what has been said and the language used' (DfEE/QCA 1999: 22).

These detailed requirements have implications for planning and organisation across the curriculum. In this book we shall explore some of these issues; discussing the learning potential of talk, considering how our planning can assist the development of children's spoken language and how we can describe and assess this development. Since the publication of *Use of Language: A Common Approach* (School Curriculum and Assessment Authority (SCAA) 1997c), which considered ways in which language and learning might be developed across the curriculum, the NLS has introduced practical approaches to raising standards in the classroom. It has become evident that speaking and listening skills underpin developments in literacy; that teaching and learning depend upon them. This fact is acknowledged in all curriculum areas in the National Curriculum (DfEE/QCA 1999) but as there is no statutory testing of speaking and listening, its status in relation to reading and writing has been less certain. Schools and teachers are less sure about how to measure progress in talk or how to develop strategies for assessment that mirror their assessment of the more permanent and observable skills of reading and writing. Office for Standards in Education (OFSTED) inspectors have also been aware that speaking and listening was not being inspected as effectively as reading and writing. It seemed that inspectors shared teachers' uncertainty about the assessment of speaking and listening. What counts as evidence of good performance and how we can develop more reliable strategies for assessment will be topics of concern in this book. It might help to begin by looking at the reasons for this uncertainty and why the need for description, analysis and assessment of speaking and listening have taken time to emerge and why what has been described as the 'richest resource' for teachers (Norman 1992: 2) can still prove problematic.

The emergence of oracy

At the start of the 1990s, a national project was under way – schools in a number of local authorities had become involved in a practical exploration of the role of talk in the classroom. Oracy was the buzzword. At nursery, primary and secondary levels, teachers, working with local and national coordinators, were embarking on uncharted territory – to create a classroom-based theory of learning centred on talk. The National Oracy Project (NOP) was to break new ground: it established new understanding and made a major contribution to the structure of English in the National Curriculum where, for the first time, Speaking and Listening was to be given equal status to Reading and Writing as attainment targets.

The National Oracy Project 1987–93

This was set up by the School Curriculum Development Committee and was administered by the National Curriculum Council (NCC). It was a curriculum development project based on action research by teachers in their classrooms. The aims of the project were to

- enhance the role of speech in the learning process 5–16 by encouraging active learning;
- develop the teaching of oral communication skills;
- develop methods of assessment of and through speech, including assessment for public examinations at 16+;
- improve pupils' performance across the curriculum;
- enhance teachers' skills and practice;
- promote recognition of the value of oral work in schools and increase its use as a means of improving learning (Norman 1992: xii).

The NOP was the natural successor to the highly successful National Writing Project (1985–88) which has had a profound effect on the understanding and practice of the teaching of writing. The Oracy Project was, however, to a large extent tackling a new aspect of learning: the importance of talk had been gradually emerging as fundamental to children's learning. It was often acknowledged implicitly but rarely made explicit in planning for the majority of curriculum subjects. The project had a powerful influence on the content and focus of the National Curriculum requirements for Speaking and Listening.

Early research 1965–76: a focus on talking and learning

The term oracy, as opposed to literacy and numeracy, emerged in the 1960s. It was coined by Andrew Wilkinson who was researching classroom talk at Birmingham University. His project was to provide early evidence of the way individuals learn through talk and particularly by working cooperatively in small groups (Wilkinson *et al.* 1965). Research carried out by Douglas Barnes in Leeds and by Harold Rosen and the London Association for the Teaching of English continued to identify classroom conditions that seemed to lead to successful learning. This led to the publication of two influential texts, *Language, the Learner and the School* (Barnes *et al.* 1969) and *From Communication to Curriculum* (Barnes 1976).

The growing evidence that pupils' learning might be enhanced by working collaboratively in small groups encouraged teachers to begin to question their reliance on a transmission model of teaching, in which they took control of what was to be learned and did most of the speaking while pupils listened. The focus shifted to considering ways of also allowing pupils to use their own language to formulate their own questions, to speculate and hypothesise about the topics and material that they were being taught. The idea that pupils might take a more active role in making sense of the curriculum began to take root. However, despite much attention to oral language and a number of research projects suggesting a variety of initiatives – in particular the use of small group work – these were slow to be taken up in schools.

A series of Her Majesty's Inspectorate (HMI) reports throughout the 1970s and early 1980s gives evidence that little attention was being paid to the development of speaking and listening. However, HMI was encouraging enthusiastic teachers to develop oral work in the classroom and by 1982 the government was giving explicit priority to curriculum development in oracy; in 1986 funding became available and plans for the NOP were finalised. At the same time, proposals to establish a National Curriculum set in motion a programme of educational reform. 'The curriculum for English was to bring speaking and listening onto the statutory agenda for every classroom' (Keiner 1992: 253). This proved to be problematic. Models of good practice and assessment were few and far between; the NOP was going to have to provide answers almost before it had begun to articulate the questions.

> Those who had worked for so long to establish a NOP could scarcely have imagined that, within months of its launch, the profession would look to it to provide rapid answers to fundamental questions about the implementation and assessment of what had suddenly become a statutory classroom requirement.
>
> (Keiner 1992: 254)

The inheritance of the NOP: a statutory classroom requirement

It is important not to underestimate the value of the early work of Douglas Barnes, Andrew Wilkinson and Harold Rosen that had put spoken language at the centre of children's learning. The emphasis may have shifted slightly from 'talking' to 'speaking', as a concern for language skills and standard English entered the literacy debate, but the interdependence of the three language modes is now taken for granted: speaking and listening is acknowledged as an integral part of learning to read and write and central to the development of literacy.

The pioneering work of the NOP teachers and coordinators in the early 1990s laid the foundations for the implementation of the Speaking and Listening requirements of the English National Curriculum and established benchmarks for practice and assessment. Its publications have provided the practical and theoretical underpinning for classrooms, teacher training and further research.

The revised National Curriculum Programmes of Study for English (DfEE/QCA 1999), as we have seen, pay considerable attention to the importance of group discussion and interaction. This new emphasis is a response to the structure of the Literacy Hour which requires pupils to work independently in small groups. They will need new skills if they are going to be able to 'talk effectively as members of a group' (DfEE/QCA 1999: 22). These skills will often need specific teaching (see Chapter 6).

Group discussion and interaction: exploratory talk

To illustrate some of the basic principles in curriculum work in oracy that were established by the NOP, we would like you to start by looking at a transcript of a group of 11-year-olds who are discussing a poem on their own. Before you read the transcript you might like to read the short poem and discuss it with a friend. It will be interesting to compare the way you thought about it with the way the boys responded. If you are able to collaborate with others it may help you to think about the value of talk in your own learning and understanding.

Looking at an example of small group talk

The transcript is a recording of four Year 6 boys who have been asked to discuss a poem, *The Small Dust-Coloured Beetle* by Robert Bloomfield. It is an eighteenth-century poem and some of the language may seem slightly obscure. See what you make of it before you discuss the boys' response.

The Small Dust-Coloured Beetle

The small dust-coloured beetle climbs with pain
O'er the smooth plantain leaf, a spacious plain!
Thence higher still, by countless steps convey'd
He gains the summit of a shivering blade,
And flirts his filmy wings, and looks around,
Exulting in his distance from the ground.

Activity

You will need about an hour to complete this activity:

- Read the poem and talk about it with colleagues. If possible, record your discussion. The boys were asked to talk about the poem and anything that it made them think about.

- Read the extract from the boys' discussion – bearing in mind that they continued to discuss this poem at greater length. Long stretches of transcript can seem daunting so read this one through to get an impression of the general strategies that are being used.

- Choose a shorter extract – say five utterances – for more detailed analysis. Looking at very small stretches of transcript in some detail can give you an insight into the way group interaction and sharing talk may enable individual discovery to take place. The following questions may help you to do this.

1. In what ways do the members of this group
   (a) support each other's contribution?
   (b) extend each other's contribution?
   (c) modify each other's contribution?

2. What is the role of the poem in this discussion?

   (a) Does it constrain or open up possibilities for discussion?

   (b) Would it have been the same sort of discussion if they had been observing a live beetle? If not, how does the fact that they are talking about a poem affect the discussion?

3. Where and how do you feel that you can see

   (a) problem solving taking place?

   (b) shared learning taking place?

Transcript: Extract from a discussion of a poem

Mark:	How does she know it's in pain? When it, where it says, 'the small dust-coloured beetle climbs with pain'. Does she know it's in pain?
Kenneth:	Ah – come on Simmy, if something's small, really, er climbing, something small to us, is very big to him, it must be tired, you've got to allow that you're going to be tired, ain't yer?
John:	Yeah, you can see what it means this poem, because it would be hard for a beetle to climb up a leaf, wouldn't it?
Mark:	It must be breathless, because the, I mean, you know, it's kind of going…
John:	Mmm
Mark:	A leaf, if it is a leaf, isn't, er, very big though, compared with a beetle
John:	No, that's true, it depends what kind of beetle it is …
Kenneth:	'Spacious plain'
John:	No – it says 'spacious plain' so it must be quite big …
Kenneth:	It is big to a beetle …
Clive:	I think the beetle must be small because not many leaves …
John:	Because there's lots of different kinds of beetles and it's probably small
Clive:	Unless it's a dock leaf, that can be pretty big
John:	or rhubarb …
Mark:	That must really, that must be hard work for a little beetle, mustn't it? 'specially that colour
Kenneth:	It is
Clive:	And beetles' legs aren't exactly the biggest
John:	Not very long
Kenneth:	Ah look, they are not very thick to us but surely they're quite thick to a beetle
John:	Yeah, you see, because if you look at, say if a beetle's …
Mark:	They'd think this is a leaf, they could easily just fly onto it … couldn't they?
John:	Yeah, it all depends whether they're winged beetles or not
Kenneth:	Yeah, why would it climb if it could fly to the top?
John:	Yeah, so it must be, it can't really be able to fly, can it?

Mark:	It must be, because look, um, 'flirts his filmy wings'
Kenneth:	Yeah, but some of these have small sort of wings, but don't fly
John:	Yeah, you look at an ostrich or a penguin
Mark:	I wonder what kind of beetle this is...it could be a ladybird, it could be any kind of beetle for all we know
John:	But there again, it could be a weak little thing that could fly down but not up
John:	Yeah, perhaps it has to have a high point to start off flying, you know, so it doesn't fall, it can't take off...
Mark:	Has to have a wind
John:	I doubt if it could fly against wind
Kenneth:	It says 'a small dust-coloured beetle'
John:	It's probably a wood beetle
Clive:	Woodlouse
John:	Yeah, woodlouse, that's right...and another thing that proves it's big it says, um...
Mark:	'By countless steps'
John:	'Thence higher still, by countless steps convey'd'
Kenneth:	And 'exulting in his distance from the ground'
John:	So, not only must the leaf be big, but the plant he's on must be quite...

Comment

You may have talked in general about the determined way that the four boys keep on task, the way that they are listening to each other, their attention to detail, their concern to establish what kind of beetle it is. They could as easily be examining a specimen under a microscope but here they are scrutinising a poem where the words offer them the clues and evidence they need.

Answering the questions above, you may have noticed:

1. (a) the way they express support for each other's ideas: *mmm...yeah...you can see what it means*

    (b) the way they extend each other's comments: Mark: *How does she know it's in pain?* Kenneth: *it must be tired*, John: *it would be hard*, Mark: *it must be breathless*

    (c) the way they modify each other's contributions: John modifies Mark's comment, *they could easily just fly onto it...couldn't they?* with, *it all depends whether they're winged beetles or not.*

Looking more closely at the interaction you may have identified some of the tentative ways they try out ideas and speculate. In the first five utterances, for example, you may have identified examples of the way they:

ask questions: *does she know it's in pain?*
speculate and hypothesise: *if something's small...it must be tired*
reason: *because it would be hard...*

give evidence: *it must be breathless because*

make assertions: *it must be tired . . . you've got to allow that*

use tags to signal tentativeness: *wouldn't it?*

tolerate each other's efforts to express an idea: *because the, I mean, you know . . .*

2. The fact that they are discussing a poem rather than observing a live beetle seems to focus their attention on the meaning of the words. They use these to support their hypothesis about the size of the beetle. Notice the way Mark, John and Kenneth quote from the text in the last four lines of the extract but at the same time draw on their experience and knowledge about insects and plants.

3. (a) and (b) You probably identified examples of problem solving and found evidence of learning taking place as they discussed the probable size of the beetle or whether it could fly, *perhaps it has to have a high point, has to have a wind, I doubt if it could fly against wind . . .*

Pupil talk and learning

Teachers working together during the NOP spent much time recording and analysing their pupils' speaking and listening. One of the conclusions that they reached was that all pupils need opportunities to work together in small groups, 'making meaning through talk, supported by their peers' (Des-Fountain and Howe 1992: 146). They drew up a set of general principles about the value of pupil–pupil talk which were based on their examination of their pupils working together. They used Barnes' theoretical exploration of the role of talk in learning to bridge the gap between theory and practice. Their principles, based on classroom evidence, support assertions that in a classroom where pupils are engaged in shared social and interactive talk:

- a readiness to learn can be created;
- pupils can work on ideas together;
- opportunities can be created for pupils to make sense of new information;
- pupils working together can provide social support for the learning process;
- tentatively expressed thoughts can become clearer in well-structured group activities.

You might like to consider the value of pupil–pupil talk. The following questions could be the basis for drawing up your own list of principles.

- How might it help pupils to talk about a task before they tackle it?
- What are the advantages of working on ideas together?
- When does it help to have the teacher in the group?
- What difference might it make if the teacher is not in the group?

You may have considered some of the following ideas:

- Through talk, pupils can recall and review what they already know and define what more they want to know about a topic.

- If pupils have already contributed their own ideas they will have a greater stake in their learning.

- Pupils who are struggling with literacy can use talk to make sense of new information.

- Ideas can be tried out to see how they sound ('How do I know what I mean until I hear what I say?').

- 'Provisional' meanings can be made as the group negotiates shared understanding.

- Tentativeness can be valued and supported because pupils are more likely to say 'I don't understand'.

- Working in a supportive peer group will help pupils to learn in the variety of English or the community language which bests suits their needs.

- Pupils can provide each other with an authentic audience, giving an immediate and engaged response which values others' contributions.

- The peer group can tolerate the need for 'thinking time' (involving social talk and silence).

- Pupils are more likely to ask each other questions in order to make meaning clearer and expand and interpret each other's ideas.

(based on Norman 1992: 144–5)

You might like to reflect on the extent to which you identified any of these principles when you were discussing the transcript of the boys talking about the poem *The Small Dust-Coloured Beetle*.

The central role of exploratory talk in cognitive development

Over the last ten years, research that grew from the activities of NOP has deepened our awareness of the power of group talk to extend intellectual development, and the ways that teachers can build this into the social context for learning in the classroom. For successful group learning to occur, teachers need to consider the relationship between the social, communicative and cognitive aspects of talking and learning and to structure tasks carefully in terms of social interdependence and cognitive demand.

Neil Mercer (2000: 1) has coined the term 'interthinking' to connect the social and cognitive functions of group talk. He describes interthinking as 'our use of language for thinking together, for collectively making sense of experience and solving problems. We do this "interthinking" in ways which most of us take for granted but which are at the heart of human achievement'.

Collaborative talk and assessment

Returning to the National Curriculum, we can see how many of the principles that emerged from curriculum development and research have been translated into the revised National

Curriculum (DfEE/QCA 1999). The Programmes of Study for English and other subjects emphasise the value of collaborative work and we need to ensure that we make space for this kind of oral work in our planning. The NOP left no doubt about the importance of Speaking and Listening across the curriculum and the value of close scrutiny of transcripts of group discussion both for diagnostic and assessment purposes.

Collecting and using evidence of talk

We are aware that there is little time for you to collect and analyse samples of pupils' talk. Pupils can be encouraged to record their own talk when working together in a group. Listening to, reflecting on and discussing their collaboration will give them the opportunity to assess their own work and to become articulate about the relationship between talk and learning. There are examples of the kinds of formats that you might use to do this in Chapter 8. Recording their own talk, in role play and drama, could also provide material for discussing the key skills such as identifying and using standard English for appropriate purposes and audiences. Speaking and Listening is perhaps the hardest of the Programmes of Study to identify and describe for assessment purposes. Writing and reading clearly permeate and underpin all curriculum subjects; it generates specific texts that can be controlled and accounted for. Speaking and listening is harder to categorise. At a general level, the National Curriculum identifies two broad areas to be taught and assessed across the English Programmes of Study: 'Knowledge, Skills and Understanding' and 'Breadth of Study'. The level descriptions for Speaking and Listening are rather generally described and assigning children to the appropriate level is hard to do with any degree of accuracy.

Assigning levels

We might try to decide which levels Mark, Kenneth, John and Clive have reached. At Level 2 children are required to be able to, 'listen carefully and respond with increasing appropriateness to what others say'. Presumably, we could safely say that from the evidence of the transcript all the boys have reached Level 2; but what else might we want to say about their performance? At Level 3 we are asked to identify whether they can, 'talk and listen confidently in different contexts'. Clearly the evidence of one transcript could not tell us whether that is the case and we would need to account for a variety of different activities over a period of time. We would also need evidence that individuals were, 'beginning to be aware of Standard English and when it is used'. Looking at the transcript, we might say that there is evidence of this, as only one non-standard form is used, 'ain't yer', and that in this informal group of friends the use of a dialect form is appropriate. The way that they quote from the poem, 'thence higher still, by countless steps convey'd' shows that they are confidently 'using a growing vocabulary' (Level 2). Using the level descriptions, we could say that as a group they have reached Level 4 (which would be appropriate for their age and stage).

> Level 4. Pupils talk and listen with confidence in an increasing range of contexts. Their talk is adapted to the purpose: developing ideas thoughtfully; describing events and conveying their opinions clearly. In discussion, they listen carefully, making contributions and asking questions that are

responsive to others' ideas and views. They use appropriately some of the features of standard English vocabulary and grammar.

(DfE 1995a)

We could confidently assign Level 4 to the group but we might feel less sure about which level to award to individual members of the group. It is through their interaction and collaboration as a group that the boys achieve Level 4 and, perhaps, learn the skills that are required to achieve Level 4. The essentially interactive and social nature of speaking and listening makes assessment difficult. However, this kind of group discussion seems to enable the participants to experience working at a higher level than they might have been able to achieve on their own. (For a broader discussion of assessment of Speaking and Listening see Chapter 8.)

Knowledge, skills and understanding: standard English and language variation

The requirements at Key Stages 1 and 2 for quite specific language study in relation to speaking and listening, suggest that teachers will have a confident understanding about the way language works. The NLS has ensured that practising teachers have received detailed and updated guidelines and more practical classroom support for the development of initiatives, such as *Grammar for Writing* (NLS 2000b) and *Developing Early Writing* (NLS 2001). It is now acknowledged that in the primary years children's knowledge about language use and structure should be developed more systematically (Bunting 2000: 19). In order to do this, teachers must also feel confident about the aspects of language that they will need to teach, understanding the structure of both spoken and written language and the way these relate to the teaching of reading, writing and speaking and listening. For many, this may mean revisiting knowledge which is almost certainly implicit or taken for granted and making it explicit; reassuring yourself that you know and can use appropriate terminology and understand how it relates to your teaching.

Making implicit knowledge (which all speakers of a language possess) explicit, is an important aspect of English work in speaking and listening in the later primary years:

Opportunities for talking about and studying language need to be ensured. These can occur in the normal, everyday work of the classroom – we need to be alert to such opportunities and to exploit them. I call these incidental opportunities. But there is a need to provide also for more focused and sustained attention to language, to set up activities, projects, sessions, where language is the central purpose. Language must take its place as part of the content of the English curriculum beyond the confines of the literacy hour.

(Bunting 2000: 20)

Speaking and Listening and the Literacy Hour

In the early stages of its implementation there was concern that the NLS framework was going to prove to be a straitjacket, that teacher talk, albeit pacy and interactive, in the form of question and answers, would limit children's responses. And to a certain extent research in 2003 and

2004 has shown this to be the case (Introduction, p. 7). Despite the claim that 'Literacy unites the important skills of reading and writing, it also involves speaking and listening which, although not separately identified in the framework, are an essential part of it' (DfEE 1998b: 3), it was clear that the framework did not include Speaking and Listening in the planning of work for literacy. The NLS framework is quite precise about the knowledge that you will need for the systematic teaching required in a dedicated Literacy Hour every day: an hour of direct instruction through 'well-paced, interactive oral work'. In the teaching of reading there is much emphasis on the systematic development of listening skills in the hour in order to identify and respond to sound patterns in language and develop phonemic awareness and phonic knowledge (DfEE/QCA 1999: En2 1a–e: 18). Stories, rhymes, alliteration and word play help pupils to hear, identify, segment and blend phonemes in words. Listening skills have a crucial role in early reading. The teaching of writing also requires speaking and listening skills – indeed these underpin all successful writing as stressed in *Developing Early Writing* (NLS 2001) and *Speaking, Listening, Learning* (QCA/DfES 2003).

Evidence from the evaluation of the early implementation of the NLS (OFSTED 1999) has shown that the teaching of reading was becoming more systematic and better structured and was leading to improved results in national tests, but that children were making slower progress in writing. As previously mentioned, the NLS has published two documents and sets of training materials to address this issue: *Grammar for Writing* (2000b), which connects sentence level objectives with teaching writing and deals with compositional skills, and *Developing Early Writing* (2001), which focuses on the teaching of writing with young children. In both, the NLS emphasises the important links between talk, writing and pupils' cognitive development:

> The growth of competence in writing also contributes importantly to the broader development of children's thinking. The more context-free and explicit nature of writing helps children to become increasingly reflective about language. By structuring and restructuring ideas in writing, children extend their powers of imagination, learn to express increasingly complex, abstract and logical relationships, and develop the skills of reasoning and critical evaluation. This, in turn, feeds back into their powers of oral communication.
>
> (NLS 2001: 8)

Ways in which the features and nature of written text are affected by oral telling and retelling of stories are discussed in Chapter 3.

Talk for writing

The DfES acknowledges the importance of the link between speech and writing in *Developing Early Writing* (NLS 2001), where it includes 'talk for writing' as part of the writing process. Talk for writing is now seen as an important feature of the NLS, 'Writing should start from talking – discussion which helps to capture content and purpose. This needs to go well beyond simply providing stimulating ideas and should help children to capture the content, sequence and style of what they are about to write' (NLS 2001: 15). Teaching units stress the role of both oral language and reading in developing writing, 'much of what children need to learn about writing from story-structure to written language features and punctuation, can be gained from story-telling, shared reading, and the oral interaction stimulated by them' (NLS 2001: 25). Talk for writing is seen as a significant feature in all aspects of the Literacy Hour; in shared writing, independent writing and plenary sessions. *Speaking, Listening, Learning: Working with Children in Key Stages 1 and 2* reinforces the link between talk and writing:

> The oral sharing of experiences and ideas supports equality of opportunity in terms of access to the curriculum and promotes children's motivation and engagement across subjects. As children's strengths and preferred learning styles differ, those children who are less comfortable and successful with written forms can communicate effectively and develop confidence through speaking and listening.
>
> (QCA/DfES 2003: 11)

Often, children are fluent speakers but struggle with writing. Teachers can consider ways of building on their oral skills to develop their writing. Kate Ruttle (2004: 73) describes how she helped Reece, a nine-year-old on the Special Educational Needs register, to become more confident as a writer. Describing Reece as a predominantly visual learner who talked fluently but seemed to find writing daunting, she capitalised on his evident storytelling skills:

> Put Reece in front of a microphone and he is in his element as a storyteller. He creates and spins yarns drawing on influences from film, TV and stories he has heard; he does accents; he modulates his voice to control the pace and atmosphere; he varies sentence structure and makes conscious use of repetition and patterning; he makes careful vocabulary choices; he shapes his stories well; he consciously adopts an authorial voice and stance.
>
> (Ruttle 2004: 73)

His teacher transcribes these stories, marks them 'in the same way as I mark all children's written work with suggestions ...' and returns them to Reece to edit and produce a final version. This has had considerable effect on Reece's confidence and understanding of the writing process. He is now working with another boy who is much less orally confident. Observing and talking with them as writers she is able to begin to understand their very different needs and to make more constructive 'notes for next step with child' as suggested on the writing task analysis sheet in the QCA criteria (QCA/DfES 2003).

As she works with the children, encouraging them to develop their writing skills, she has come to understand that

> the process of dialogic talk underpins all their learning – not just their learning as writers ... Promoting and encouraging dialogic talk helps children to understand and express their own 'personal constructs'. Through this, they begin to understand their learning, which in turn, helps teachers to understand the children as writers and so to undertake purposeful assessment for learning.
>
> (Ruttle 2004: 77)

Dialogic talk is a way to access children's understanding of texts and also of the meaning they ascribe to teachers' instructions.

This is the case when working with children like Reece who have special needs as it is with children who are particularly gifted. The QCA publication and video, *Working with Gifted and Talented Children: Key Stages 1 and 2 English and Mathematics* (QCA 2001), gives exemplification and is a useful resource.

Teacher–pupil talk

The NOP not only increased our understanding of talk and learning as an interactive and collaborative activity, but also focused among others on issues of bilingualism, gender, teacher–pupil talk and the discourse of different subject disciplines. This takes us back to the snail transcript introduced at the beginning of this chapter that highlighted the need to monitor and listen to ourselves as speakers. There has been much discussion of the function of questioning in the classroom: we are all familiar with the kind of questions that require pupils to make inspired guesses about what the teacher has in mind, the questions that test whether they have been paying attention or remember information that they have already been taught. These are often single-answer questions of a closed kind that do not invite or require speculation but are necessary to establish a shared use of terminology or the specialist vocabulary required by a particular activity or subject. The teacher in the snail transcript illustrates this:

Teacher:	What is the snail doing with the bottom horns?
Susan:	He is feeling along the ground
Teacher:	He's feeling along, so what would you call the bottom horns, Jason?
Susan:	Arms? No ... sort of ...
Emma:	Legs?
Teacher:	You think they're legs, you think they're arms. What do you think they are, Jason, if he's feeling with them?
Jason:	Feelers

This is a common strategy that is frequently used to establish the terminology that is being used in a particular curriculum area.

With the introduction of a ten-subject National Curriculum there has been a concern for more specialist teaching. The Speaking and Listening Orders specifically require that pupils should be able to use spoken language for a range of purposes: to tell stories, explore, develop and clarify, predict, discuss, describe, observe, explain and reason, ask and answer questions while working in groups of different sizes and presenting work to different audiences. Working in different contexts it is expected that they will become aware of the range of choices that they must make in different situations. Through speaking and listening activities they will begin to become aware of and use a range of different registers.

At Key Stage 2 there is more emphasis on making these choices explicit as pupils use grammatical structures and vocabulary that are specific to the genre or style used by different subjects. At this stage, they need to be taught more specifically how to organise what they want to say and to 'use vocabulary and syntax that enables them to communicate more complex meanings' (DfEE/QCA 1999: 22).

Working in small groups has an important role to play in achieving this; through group discussion and interaction the range of purposes for pupils at Key Stage 2 should include investigating, selecting, sorting; planning, predicting, exploring; explaining, reporting, evaluating (DfEE/QCA 1999: En1 10a–c: 22).

The National Curriculum requires that from Key Stage 1 pupils should be introduced to a wide range of texts including print and information and communications technology (ICT) based information texts, reading for information in non-fiction and non-literary texts. They should also be encouraged to write appropriately for a range of different audiences and be able to organise and explain information. They can discuss these texts both at whole-class level, where the teacher can model and encourage dialogic talk, and in small groups; Guided Reading in the Literacy Hour can be an ideal time for this.

The NLS recognises that moving from informal everyday language to being able to handle the discourse of the subject discipline does not happen spontaneously and the framework provides specific strategies that will enable pupils to cope with an increasingly wide range of non-fiction genre. In *Grammar for Writing* (NLS 2000b) there is a summary of the organisation and language features of non-fiction texts, and units of work demonstrate how pupils may develop an increasingly sophisticated grasp of the grammatical structures required for non-fiction writing.

> Like the child's conversational learning of and through language in the pre-school years, learning in school can be seen quite largely as a continuing apprenticeship in discourse, as he or she participates in, and takes over, the different discourse genres – that is, ways of making meaning – that are encountered in various subjects of the curriculum.
>
> (Wells 1992: 291)

The children in the two transcripts that you have looked at are in the early stages of this apprenticeship. The younger group talking about the snails have learned the basic rules of collaboration – listening and turn-taking, hypothesising and speculating – but they are using mainly cumulative talk (see Chapter 6) and will need more help from the teacher to use more confident exploratory talk. The 11-year-olds discussing a poem have come a lot further; they are handling and sharing evidence. Both groups had learned how to do this through experiencing this kind of activity in a variety of ways in their classrooms; their teachers had laid the foundations for them to be able to engage in the discourse of the specialist subjects they are going to be required to use.

Valuing individuals: diversity and inclusion

The National Curriculum has a concern for diversity and inclusion in all areas of the curriculum; all children need to be able to use the English language for a variety of purposes if they are to have equal opportunity within our schools and society. However, for pupils who are acquiring English as an additional language (EAL) opportunities can seem less than equal. The SCAA (1996a) document *Teaching English as an Additional Language: A Framework for Policy* addresses this issue, establishing a set of key principles. It makes clear the responsibilities that all teachers have for teaching English as well as subject content, 'the teaching of effective spoken and written English needs to be embedded in the teaching and learning of subject content' (SCAA 1996a: 7). It stresses that an aim in teaching EAL is to 'build on the knowledge of other languages and cultures' (SCAA 1996a: 2) and outlines the need to develop whole-school policies. The English Programmes of Study (DfEE/QCA 1999: 49) allow specific attention to be given to the needs of EAL learners and provide opportunities for focused work on language. The NLS has provided specific training materials for class teachers for raising the attainment of minority ethnic pupils (*Supporting Pupils Learning English as an Additional Language* (NLS 2000a)). The emphasis is on the importance of developing spoken English as a prerequisite for the development of all other skills.

Gender issues

This chapter has suggested some of the issues that you will need to be aware of and think about as you plan schemes of work for Speaking and Listening. If you are going to help all children to participate equally in a curriculum that values oracy, there will be many more that you will need to take into account and often these relate specifically to individuals or groups in your classroom. For example, we need to be aware of and sensitive to gender differences in speaking and listening. By the time children come to school they have already learned how to speak in different ways according to their gender and their gendered identities (Swann 1992). You will need to take gender into consideration in your planning and assessment. As *Speaking, Listening, Learning* (QCA/DfES 2003: 12) reminds us:

> Characteristics of the talk of boys and girls often differ. Girls are generally more collaborative, supporting each other and developing ideas together. Boys often like to propose ideas, to use language dramatically and to move on fast rather than develop detail.

As Browne (1996: 182) suggests:

> By aiming to free children from the constraints of gender and taking positive steps to cater for the different needs of girls and boys as learners of English, teachers are helping to create opportunities for greater achievement across the curriculum for all pupils they teach.

Conclusion

Over the last 30 years, what began as a specialist research topic on children's spoken language has broadened to an understanding of the interrelationship in learning and teaching between speaking and listening, reading and writing. Oracy is now fully integrated as one of the three Programmes of Study for English in the National Curriculum. The pressure for change that led to this came from a curriculum project that was based in actual classroom practice where teachers were able to explore and reflect together. We hope that this book will encourage groups of teachers in training and in classrooms to continue to talk and reflect together about their experience and practice.

For the team writing this book, we have become more aware of the capacity of speaking and listening to be central to the objectives of a society that values life-long learning in a participative democracy. The process starts in the home with the development of the child's own language resources in social interaction with family and community, is promoted through constructive strategies at the start of formal learning (see Chapter 2), is recognised in diagnostic baseline assessment (see Chapter 8) and ultimately leads to the self-managing, independent, autonomous adult, confidently using language as a citizen.

Further reading

Corden, R. (2000) *Literacy and Learning Through Talk: Strategies for the Primary Classroom.* Buckingham: Open University Press.

Mercer, N. (2000) *Words and Minds: How we use language to think together.* London: Routledge.

2

Talk in the Early Years

Lorraine Hubbard

Introduction: from home to school

I can remember when I first took a Reception class complaining to a colleague about the 'poor' language of the children in my class, 'Why, they can't even ask to go to the toilet properly', I grumbled. 'Well', Martin replied somewhat carefully, 'I don't know about you, but in our house we don't *ask* to go to the toilet, we just go.' Although my first reaction was to laugh, my inward reaction was one of mild indignation. My expectation, perfectly laudable, was that the child, after raising her hand, should say 'Please Mrs Hubbard, may I go to the toilet?' As their teacher I was there to help the children, many from a deprived socio-economic background, to achieve and one of the best ways of doing this was to encourage them to speak 'properly' as soon as possible in order to reach the level of literacy that I wanted for them. On speaking to other Reception class teachers I found that their complaints echoed mine. We wanted the children to succeed academically and at the same time to speak clearly, succinctly and to the point, preferably in sentences, and with socially appropriate language. What we wanted was a culturally specific language reflecting our own backgrounds as teachers, and if the child did not match this then they and their parents were regarded as deficient in some way. Parents were censured in particular – after all where had the children been the last five years?

On reflection, I think that my colleague Martin's remark prompted me for the first time to consider the context of the shift from home to school for four- or five-year-olds and the language implications of this change of environment. In 1985 when I was teaching in Devon, I was keen to take part in a study of young children's talk at home and at school. As part of my preparation I read a book by Tizard and Hughes, *Young Children Learning* (1984), which turned out to be a critical event in my teaching career. I realised that my linguistic demands of the children were wholly inappropriate and that my knowledge of language development was quite inadequate. I began to realise that I knew very little about the home life of my children and that what knowledge I had was based on assumptions. It was only on visiting children at home and talking to their parents that I began to gain a more realistic picture of their language and the real language ability of the children in my class.

Aim of this chapter

This chapter aims to reassert the value and importance of talk, drawing on good practice by teachers working with young children in their classrooms. It is about speaking and listening being an essential part of the development of literacy. Teachers, particularly in the light of the Literacy Hour, do not necessarily have to change their activities radically in order to develop speaking and listening. What this chapter seeks to do is to help teachers revisit and reflect on the power of talk in day-to-day life in the early years classroom.

Talk in the early years

Any understanding of the way children and adults use language at home and at school must be grounded in the ways in which language itself develops and in the very nature of talk. You may find it useful to think of conversation and speaking and listening as analogous to a game of tennis. The talk itself is the tennis ball and the speaker and listener the two players. The server/speaker hits the talk to the receiver/listener who then becomes the hitter/speaker and hits the talk back to the server/receiver. This toing and froing continues until perhaps the ball falls short (a misunderstanding/unclear explanation), when one of the players has to reach out and retrieve it, before hitting the talk back into the play area/conversation and so the game continues. Talk between an adult and a young child is analogous to a game of ball with a toddler. The adult has to do most of the work running round and retrieving the ball (or talk) and practically throwing the ball (or talk) into the arms (or ears) of the less experienced player (or talker). I do not think it is claiming too much to assert that playing like this with a toddler is almost a natural reaction. It is Davies (Wilkinson *et al.* 1991: 111) who writes that 'speech is part of normal behaviour' yet this very ease and naturalness of use can lead us to underestimate its importance in language and learning. Talk is not like reading and writing, which are taught explicitly by teachers, having high status and being systematically recorded in the classroom. But we do not explicitly teach talk in the classroom and it is an arduous process to record and transcribe. It is perhaps the transitory nature of talk which makes it difficult to track, to assess and comment upon.

Talk in the home

The richness of talk in the home has been well researched and documented, most notably by Brice-Heath (1983), Tizard and Hughes (1984), Wells (1987) and in the *Early Years Language Project* in Devon which started work in 1986. A typical transcript from this project reveals a four-year-old in conversation with his mother. The family lived in a dockland area of a major city and spoke in the local dialect. In this extract the mother is explaining to four-year-old Ross that he will be eating school dinners when he starts school shortly.

R: You do have to buy me a packed lunch box 'cos I go packed lunch.

M: Well you'll stay to dinners like Neil. (*His brother*)

R: That's school dinners.

M: That's school dinners like Neil, won't yer?

R: Yeah, an' you goin' 'ave to buy me a box.

M: Oh no, you won't need a packed lunch box if you staying school dinners 'cos they'll cook yer dinner in school an' give it to yer.

R: No they don't 'cos they 'aven't got a cooker.

M: They have.

R: You wouldn't know.

M: Yeah.

R: You gotta make it.

M: No, Mummy don't make it, they make it in school an' then you sit down with all the other children an' eat yer dinner.

Later in the same conversation they are talking about Ross starting school:

M: Yeah, well, that's what you go to school for to learn how to write things down and how to read and how to spell, i'n'it?

R: You can't spell.

M: Can.

R: No you can't.

M: I can.

R: When you was four you couldn't spell.

M: No, that's why Mummy went to school, to learn, that's why you go to school, i'n'it?

R: To learn.

M: Mmm.

R: Did you go to school to learn?

M: Mmm.

R: You don't now do you?

M: No, don't go t'school now.

Ross and his mother are using the language of their speech community to further Ross's knowledge about school. It is an example of what Tizard and Hughes (1984) would call 'a passage of intellectual search', an example of speech they found to be all too rare in the nursery school. Ross, by making challenging statements, is trying to make sense of an important aspect of school life. His mother, in her explanations, is attempting to reassure him and clear up his misunderstandings about school dinners. Ross and his mother are communicating well and 'the basics' are there. What we need to remember is that home talk might well be different but it is not deficient. The Bullock Report, *A Language for Life*, urged that 'No child should be expected to cast off the language and culture of the home, as she crosses the threshold nor to act as though school and home represent two totally separate and different cultures, which have to be kept firmly apart' (DES 1975: 286).

Activity

Is the language spoken in this extract different from what we would expect in school? In what ways? Perhaps you feel that there is a more even 'balance of power' between the two speakers. Because of the close relationship between mother and child there are more one-word answers and sometimes these are not conventional words, but ones they use when they are together. The child is exploring something that puzzles him. Would he be able to do this in a busy classroom?

Into school

Of course teachers cannot attempt to replicate the one-to-one conversation which happens in the home, yet if the 'basics' of communication are there, teachers are well able to build on these. The *Curriculum Guidance for the Foundation Stage* (DfEE/QCA 2000) sets out its aims on language and communication in the Early Learning Goals and refers specifically to speaking and listening: 'Conversation, open-ended questions and thinking out loud are important tools in developing vocabulary and in challenging thinking' (DfEE/QCA 2000: 23). Further guidance is given in the stepping stones. Children with English as an additional language are specifically addressed, as is the importance of building on their language experiences at home.

For example, a popular topic with young children is 'Ourselves'. A good starting point for this is for the teacher to bring in a photograph of herself as a baby and tell stories of her own family. The next step is for the children to bring into school photographs of themselves when they were babies and any toys, clothes or books that might still be in the family. Topics like this are rich in learning potential and often expand to include parents and other areas of the curriculum. Their great strength is that they build on the child's own background, knowledge and experience. It is important to focus on the spoken language and although a great deal of talk occurs naturally in an early years classroom, it is useful and fun to have specific lessons on talking about talk. You might ask the children to consider the kinds of language they used when they were very young.

- How did you ask for a drink when you were a baby?
- What did you use for 'thank you' and 'please'?
- What do you say now?
- How do you ask for a drink at school?
- How do you greet your friends/teacher/head teacher?
- Can we write it down? What do you notice?

It is important to write these down on a large sheet of paper in order to draw attention to the words or phrases. A simple table could be drawn up in order to discuss family words sometimes called 'idiolect' and their orthodox equivalents:

	1 year	5 years
mother	maaa	mum
father	daaa	dad

Such tables can be made more complex by the addition of more words and ages: they can be individual tables or a whole-class activity. The teacher with skill and sensitivity enables the children to reflect on their idiolect and perhaps on the wider issues of speaking and writing, for example this is what we all *say*, but what would we *write*? Particular aspects that need to be addressed are adaptation to listeners and context and an introduction to some of the features that distinguish standard English from the patterns of speech practised so far by the child.

The issue here is that the children are talking about the language itself, they are learning about language through talking about language and acquiring a metalanguage. As teachers are surrounded by constant talk in a busy Reception class, it is easy to forget its importance; there's a danger of not giving talk its due attention. Speaking and listening are not incidental but require definite planning.

Activity

What would be our specific aims for speaking and listening in a topic on 'Ourselves'? You may have considered the following: reflection on our own talk, the differences between speaking and writing, the recognition of the differences in talk and what is appropriate at different times. Of course, any aims would also need to take into account the Programmes of Study.

News time

This is a classic activity in early years classrooms, with children gathered on the carpet in front of the teacher. It is used for an exchange of news, 'show and tell', story or the re-enforcement of a specific point the teacher wants to get across. Many teachers, believing it to be a time for children to express themselves orally, gave it considerable time. More recent research – the National Oracy Project (NOP) (1989–93), for example – suggests that news time in practice is often an opportunity for the teacher rather than the children to talk, and that its value for the development of children's talk can be limited. A variant of news time is sometimes called circle time, which incorporates a more personal approach and encourages children to express their feelings on particular issues. Other observers (Housego and Burns 1994) question the appropriateness of this more personal form of interaction in the context of British cultural norms. And yet many are convinced of the value of gathering together on the carpet for the purpose of stimulating speaking and listening. Children are often bursting to relate a recent event or to show a new toy, and teachers need to give information while children need to listen. We should re-examine the usefulness of circle time and how it might be used more effectively:

- in pairs or groups, children can exchange news
- a 'jigsaw' (see Howe 1997: 20) in which children, after hearing each other's news, change groups and retell
- a feedback point, i.e. stopping the class in order to draw their attention to a specific item or to highlight similar events
- holding a much-loved toy while speaking.

None of these ideas is new but we need to evaluate what is perhaps a routine practice and try to discover the 'strange in the familiar'. In other words, we should re-examine the learning potential of news time and rediscover why the sharing of experience through talk is so valuable.

Activity

Can we think of other ways of using this time? What should the teacher's role be? Among your considerations think of the teacher as a facilitator, a listener and an observer. You might also want to question whether or not we are justified in asking children to express their feelings in public and what do we do if a child is reluctant to air her feelings?

Puppets

The possibilities for talk, not just in the making of puppets but in their presentation, are very wide ranging, and can help to widen the children's talk repertoire. Children for whom English is an additional language are able to use puppets as a vehicle for speaking in their first language as well as their second. A book is a useful starting point, preferably a well-known story so that the children can 'roam around the known', explore the story and make it their own (Clay 1979: 55). For example *Topiwalo* is a traditional Indian tale with a simple storyline. It tells of an old hatmaker who encounters a group of cheeky monkeys on his way to market to sell his hats. The monkeys steal the hats and the story goes on to relate how Topiwalo tricks the monkeys into giving them back. A dual language book can be useful in this context for highlighting similarities and differences between two languages. What we need to consider are the stages in such a topic, which might be:

- a reading of the story in English/community language
- looking at the differences in the writing of the two languages
- a retelling of the story in English/community language
- tape-recording the children telling stories in English/community language
- including a rhythmic or musical accompaniment, e.g. Indian drums
- telling related traditional stories

- making of simple puppets, e.g. pea sticks and paper plates
- last, but not least, arranging a presentation to an audience.

The exploration of first language with bilingual children is important in order to give status and credibility to the first language and culture. This is important not only to the bilingual speakers but also the English monolingual children. The gains in confidence from any kind of presentation are crucial, but this might also be a presentation involving parents or classroom assistants. We know also from the work of David (1990) and Siraj-Blatchford (1994) that the encouragement of the child's first language has a direct bearing on the success with which she develops a second language. Furthermore, as the child grows in confidence in her second language, the balance between the two languages has the potential to provide further cognitive benefits (Mills and Mills 1993) and can lead to the development of interlanguage. This is a term used to refer to the child's own language system which develops through use and experimentation. This can also occur during the process of the movement back and forth between two or more languages which in its turn develops new knowledge and understandings. An issue for the monolingual English teacher is how to track and assess a child who is speaking in a language she does not understand. The use of other community language users such as teachers, nursery nurses, assistants and parents can be invaluable here.

Learning through talk may bring benefits in other areas of the curriculum. In the case quoted, the making of the puppets raised issues to do with art and technology. The range of talk involved in such a piece of work deserves analysing in the light of statutory requirements. Specific areas addressed include:

- telling stories
- participating in a performance, using appropriate language
- listening
- speaking clearly and with confidence
- a consideration of audience.

Making puppets also involved talk in relation to problem solving, including questioning, explaining, justifying, reasoning and hypothesising.

However, there are other aspects to traditional tales such as *Topiwalo*. Many of the traditional stories are highly moral and can be used as a resource to cover various aspects of the curriculum. Bearing in mind current OFSTED demands, we need to look at the wider aspects of such stories and how we can address important issues. The inspectors are required to report on the spiritual, moral, social and cultural development of pupils and how effectively the school teaches cultural diversity. These requirements are also echoed in the Early Learning Goals, particularly in personal, social and emotional development and also in the National Curriculum. One way of addressing these demands is through story. A few examples of such stories which raise these issues are *The Six Blind Men and the Elephant* by H. Hester, *Fourteen Rats and a Rat-catcher* by Tamasin Cole and James Cressey, *Granpa* by John Burningham, *The Great Big Enormous Turnip* by Alexei Tolstoy (see Baumfield 1996).

Activity

How would a story address the spiritual, moral, social and cultural aspects of the curriculum? Can you identify the speaking and listening element? The list of books above takes into account issues such as a death in the family, working together to achieve a goal and listening to the opinions of others. For further work and ideas on story see *Start with a Story* (Sylvester 1991) and *Making Sense of a New World* (Gregory 1996).

Problem solving

'Investigations and problem-solving activities are efficient in helping pupils to apply and extend their learning in new contexts' (OFSTED 1995: 69). As teachers we are aware of this already but as it has been made explicit by OFSTED perhaps we need to consider how we can address it explicitly in the classroom. One way is through group collaborative talk (see Chapter 6). Collaborative talk in order to solve a science or technology problem is an example of children using talk in order to learn. Often in these contexts the nature of the talk is untidy, for example sentences will be unfinished, words repeated, and considerable interruptions will take place. Children need to be in groups for this kind of activity and it must be a task which requires them to talk to each other.

The classification game

- Give each group plenty of small pieces of paper and a topic each – animals, plants, food, TV programmes. Each group should not know the topic titles you have given to the other groups.
- Each group writes down examples of the category on the separate pieces of paper. For example, the animals group would write down the name of an animal on each piece of paper.
- The group sorts and then classifies the names. *You would need to ask the group why they have organised their examples in this way.*
- Exchange papers with another group. *Will this group classify differently? Can they guess the title you gave the other group?*

Activity

How would you bring this activity to a conclusion? You might find it useful to draw together the whole class in order to reflect on their decisions and relate the game to their current history or geography work.

The pin-eating animal game (See Figure 2.1)

This is a problem-solving activity devised by a BEd student at the University of Exeter, which again needs the children to work in groups.

- Give out the picture of the body of the pin-eating animal and the various feet, tails and heads to match.
- The children next have to decide which head, feet, tail are the most appropriate for the body of the pin-eating animal as he travels through the forest.

There is of course no right answer – which in itself is a learning experience – but the level of reasoning, justifying, speculating, hypothesising, specifying and persuading is considerable from this kind of task. However, this is an activity that is worth further exploration and analysis. Why would we do such a lesson in terms of the National Curriculum? The aim would be to widen the children's talk repertoire and improve their communication skills and an activity such as this would encourage the children to communicate effectively. They would need to choose their words in order to justify their standpoint and to learn the conventions of discussion, e.g. turn-taking. Through talk the children would develop their thinking and extend their ideas through discussion.

We also need to consider other aspects which constitute good practice and which OFSTED would note, such as classroom organisation and management, differentiation, assessment, use of time and resources, and the expectations by the teacher of the children.

Activity

What would be the teacher's role in this activity? For example, as well as listening and observing, there would be times during the activity when you would need to intervene. The drawing together of the group discussions could provide a useful forum.

The Noisy Poems

This kind of activity can be done with a range of poems and is very useful, especially if the class has an assembly performance looming! While working with student teachers I have used poetry from the book *Noisy Poems* edited by Jill Bennett (1987), which includes a wide range of noises from clanking trains and vociferous jazz bands to the softness of fish fins and the gentle sound of sampans in the water.

- Give each group several copies of a poem, each group to have a different poem.
- Each group is to give a presentation of their particular poem. This will include actions and sound effects.
- Their first audience will naturally be each other, but if a performance standard is required then several rehearsals and refinements will be necessary.

This can be a noisy lesson! However, it is useful to reflect on the kinds of learning going on.

In the forest where he lives the pin trees are loaded with heavy crops of pins. His enemies creep up behind him to attack.

FIGURE 2.1 The pin-eating animal game

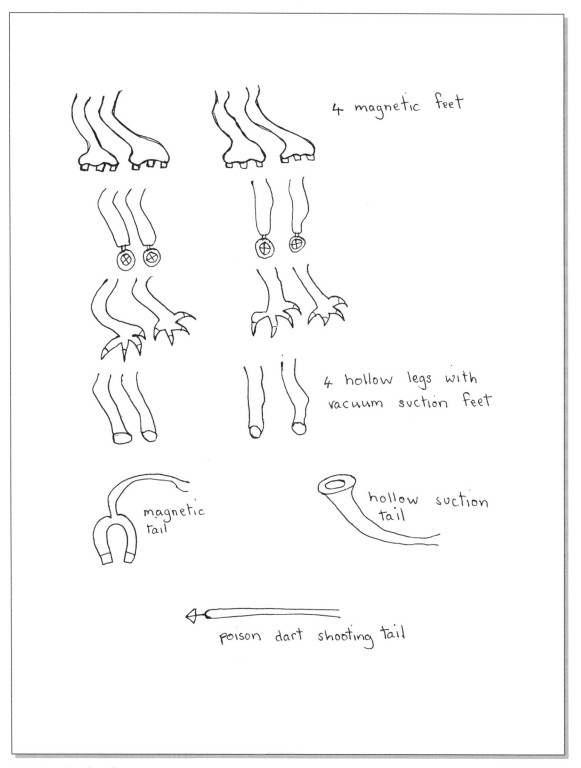

FIGURE 2.1 (continued)

Activity

The head teacher is showing a parent governor around the school and the governor expresses surprise later at the amount of talk being allowed. How would you explain your lesson? You might, for example, refer to the National Curriculum and the aims of the lesson, but perhaps most importantly – invite the governor to the performance!

The child as a powerful thinker

A student teacher from De Montfort University, while working with Reception children on the story of Noah, asked one child where she thought Noah sailed to. The child with unanswerable logic replied, 'They sailed to Tesco, because they had no food.' Many a teacher has a fund of stories like this which are retold as amusing anecdotes and to illustrate a naive logic. Yet this logic is also evidence of powerful and logical thinking at work in relation to the child's own cultural experience.

It was Vygotsky whose work taught us that the child has the capacity, with help, to develop ideas or concepts beyond their current level and that children are able to act and think with understanding of another point of view. *Children's Minds* (Donaldson 1978) was one of the books which first alerted us to the intellectual powers of the young child and was critical of the Piagetian view of the child as intellectually egocentric, a view which had a strong hold for many years over the minds of educators in early years classrooms. The work of Tizard and Hughes (1984) enlightened us further on the child as a powerful thinker; they describe children coming to terms with abstract ideas through talk. These powers need to be exercised and developed through talk in order for the child to gain control over their thinking and to make their thoughts explicit. The recent European Human Rights Act legislation of 2000 raised an awareness of children's rights and needs so that there are additional protocols currently underway which will amend the 1989 United Nations Convention for the Rights of the Child. Basically children have a fundamental right to be consulted on what is happening in their lives and in an article in *Practical Pre-School* (Issue 27; Update June 2001) attention is drawn to the work of Alison Clark and Peter Moss at the Thomas Coram Research Unit and Sterling Council Children's Service on consulting children on matters concerning their education (Price 2001). This will involve discussions with children on issues such as resources, their routines and activities. Obviously the young child does not possess the relevant experience and skills in order to make sophisticated decisions and long-lasting statements, but they can benefit by interacting with an adult.

Tina Bruce (1997) devotes a chapter of her book to 'The ability of the child to decentre'. Bruce explains that the child can empathise with others and is capable of understanding a point of view other than their own. Yet there are situations when the adult is needed in order to take the child further in their thinking: 'The role of the early childhood educator seems to be that of a bridge from embedded to disembedded tasks, from everyday meanings to situations beyond the immediate here and now' (Bruce 1997: 135). In other words the child is not intellectually incompetent but inexperienced. What the child needs is help to do things which they cannot do on their own.

Although children will display throughout the day evidence of their reasoning and understanding, it is also valuable to plan for specific activities for children to 'clarify their understanding and indicate thoughtfulness about the matter under discussion' (OFSTED 1995: 4). Specific activities might be:

1. Provocative statements displayed in a corner of the classroom can be used in order to encourage discussion, for example:

   ■ Children should wear their school uniform every day.

   ■ Children should only be allowed sweets at the weekend.

   ■ Children should go to school on a Saturday.

   I have seen these titles put up in the writing corner in order to encourage argumentative writing after the discussion. Yet they can also stand alone as a talking activity.

2. Negotiating rules of behaviour in the classroom is a way in which many teachers encourage good behaviour. This negotiation through talk is meant to enforce good discipline in school through the children having some input themselves. Another aspect of this can be the children negotiating 'rules of talk' in the classroom (see Chapter 6). This is another useful way of talking about talk and of reinforcing positive and appropriate rules of conduct.

3. Stories can be a useful bridge. Moral tales such as *Aesop's Fables* have long been used by teachers in order to instil good behaviour in their pupils, but we can and should broaden out these discussions to include moral issues of the day. There are a host of stories and books which can act as starting points or springboards for this kind of activity – furthermore, they can raise issues in an accessible way, often through humour.

   Particular works and authors to note are:

   ■ Anthony Browne, especially *Gorilla* which encourages children to 'read' the pictures.

   ■ John Burningham's *Would You Rather?* encourages children to think and reach a decision.

   ■ The poems of Charles Causley, such as *I Saw A Jolly Hunter* and *My Mother Saw A Dancing Bear*, raise issues such as hunting and cruelty to animals.

   ■ Jan Ormerod's *Chicken Licken* is a delight, a picture book incorporating two stories.

Other authors/titles and topic areas

J. Baker	*Window*. Environmental issues
S. and J. Berenstein	*He Bear, She Bear*. Looking at gender roles
Anne Fine	*Bill's New Frock*. Gender roles
Michael Foreman	*Dinosaurs and all that Rubbish*. Environmental issues
Hoffman and Binch	*Amazing Grace*. Gender and race

Pat Hutchins	*Rosie's Walk*. Survival issues
Arnold Lobel	*Owl at Home.* A collection of apparently humorous stories which have deeper meaning. *The Frog and Toad Stories* which explore friendship
Jenny Wagner	*John Brown, Rose and the Midnight Cat*. Issues of jealousy

What sort of questions?

We need to be flexible to children's responses to a story yet, because of our awareness of the importance of talk, we also need to plan some of the questions we could ask. This planning would avoid the trap of asking questions such as, 'What colour is the cat?' or 'How many elephants can you see?' These questions have their place, but they are closed questions and unlikely to stimulate thinking.

The conversations which challenge thinking as advocated in *Curriculum Guidance for the Foundation Stage* (DfEE/QCA 2000) have also been researched by Mercer (2003) and Alexander (2004). While sequences of Alexander's dialogic talk are not necessarily easy to achieve in the early years classroom, all children nevertheless need 'involvement in thoughtful and reasoned dialogue' (Mercer 2003: 76) which should become a part of their oral repertoire. An example of the beginnings of this can be seen in the QCA/DfES (2003) video (*Speaking, Listening, Learning: Working with Children in Key Stages 1 & 2* (2003)) towards the end of the sequence showing the teacher questioning the child in a science activity in a Key Stage 1 classroom. The recent work of Larson and Peterson (2003: 309) sums this up when they write that:

> on the whole, [these] researchers agree that early childhood educators should give children ample opportunities to participate in extended discourse forms, including narratives, explanations, pretend talk, and other forms of complex conversations, in order to achieve successful school-based outcomes.

On reflection I think some guidelines are needed, such as opening questions of the type 'Can you tell me what you have been doing?' Then, of course, we need to listen to the child's answer. This might sound obvious to many, but during the course of a busy day in the classroom it is easy to forget, especially as talk is the easiest, most used and most accessible form of communication.

The help that teachers give to children in order to further their learning is often called scaffolding, a term coined by Bruner. But Eve Gregory (1996: 21) warns us that, as learning is different across cultures, so the scaffolding we provide should also take account of this difference. Cathy Nutbrown (1994: 75) in discussing the role of the teacher writes:

> Part of the responsibility of teachers and other educators is to ensure that children hear a wide range of talk and terminology and can therefore generate the words they need to be able to talk about their own findings and communicate their important and developing ideas through language.

Activity

Take some of the books from the list above and try to think of some questions you might ask your class. *Tell Me* by Aidan Chambers (1992) is a useful resource on which to base your questions and below are some suggestions adapted from his book:

■ Could you present this book/activity to the class? How?

■ What will you tell your friends about this book/activity?

■ What kind of book/story did you think it was going to be?

■ What is the most important thing about this story/activity?

■ Would you like to read/do this again? If yes: would you read/do it differently?

Language play

Rhyme has long been regarded as a key tool in developing children's literacy, but the work of Bryant and Bradley (1985) and Goswami and Bryant (1990) has alerted us to the importance of rhyme in phonological awareness, that is the ability to reflect on sounds in words. What has developed from this work is the need to be explicit in drawing children's attention to rhyme, the sounds of words and their spelling.

Playing with the sounds of rhyme is the beginning of sound awareness in young children. My Reception class used to love *Mrs Wishy-Washy* from the Storychest Series and would often chant 'wishy-washy, ishy-oshy, pishy-poshy' or variations thereof. One of the joys of Michael Rosen's *We're Going on a Bear Hunt* is the 'splash! splosh!' and the 'swishy! swashy!' accompanied by appropriate actions. The poetry and playfulness of language, the 'savouring' (Beard 1995: 7) of the sounds of the words in the mouth, is of principal importance in the early years. This leads on to the more sophisticated play on language encountered in Margaret Mahy's books, for example, do we make explicit the pleasure of the aunt's 'delicious rumblebumpkins' in *The Horrendous Hullabaloo* or the magical feel of 'the drift and the dream of it, the weave and the wave of it, the fume and foam of it' from *The Man Whose Mother was a Pirate?* The exotic names such as Novosti Krovsky in John Burningham's *Where's Julius?* or the seemingly nonsensical 'zoodle oop, little Zog' from Sarah Williams' *Good Zap, Little Grog* also provide a source of pleasure as well as the beginnings of sound awareness. But apart from an exaggerated reading or rereading of some of the passages, I would not attempt to explain away the enjoyment.

The rhythm and the repetition found in much early years poetry also helps along the sound. Early examples of this are the nursery rhymes children hear from a very early age. A later example might be Clive Sansom's 'The Song of the Train'. It would be extremely difficult not to be carried away – linguistically speaking – by the 'clickitty clack, clickitty-clack, this is the way we begin the attack'.

Tongue-twisters are another form of language play and they can be exploited to draw attention to initial sounds. Children enjoy the alliteration and can invent them easily.

Alphabet dictionaries on a variety of themes can be made with children, e.g. Alex adores apples, Balbir bakes biscuits, Colin cooks cakes, etc. Other early encounters with language play are the playground rhymes that have been collected in works such as Opie and Opie (1959).

The chanting in the playground of the somewhat aggressive:

> I'm the king of the castle
> Geroff! You dirty rascal!

to the rather more gentle

> Oh, I'm a little Dutch girl a Dutch girl a Dutch girl
> Oh, I'm a little Dutch girl from over the sea.

The appeal of the strong rhythm, the rhyme, the easy repetition and the downright subversiveness (see Grugeon 1988) of these playground chants might appear obvious, but these early experiences are valuable. They give children an introduction to aspects of literature and it is this combination of rhyme, repetition and rhythm that helps the sound of the language to become memorable and form a basis for literacy.

Other authors/titles

V. Aardema	*Bimwili and the Zimwi.*
Lynley Dodd	*Hairy Maclary from Donaldson's Dairy.*
Wanda Gag	*Millions of Cats.*
Gail E. Haley	*A Story, A Story.*
Dr Seuss	*Fox in Socks.*

Rhyme and rhythm

Working with rhyme is a long-established part of the experience of young children in the development of literacy. It is perhaps the particular work of Goswami and Bryant (1990) that has highlighted the importance of aspects of rhyme such as onset and rime. These are linguistic terms and are explained in Goswami (1994). Put simply, a syllable can be divided into two units: the onset and the rime. The onset in the syllable is the initial consonant(s). The rime is the vowel(s) and any following consonants in the syllable. The following table (adapted from James 1996) explains this further.

Word	Syllable	Onset	Rime
cat	cat	c	at
stream	stream	str	eam
midnight	mid	m	id
	night	n	ight

Before children begin school they have an awareness of rhyme that can be used as a resource in learning to read through work on onset and rime. A good beginning can be poetry, e.g. 'Chicken and chips' (Anon) from *A Packet of Poems* (Oxford University Press 1982).

> Chicken and chips,
> Chicken and chips,
> Everyone here likes chicken and chips.
> We eat them all day
> Never throw them away
> We all like chicken and chips.

Read the children the whole poem asking them to join in and then invent other words to rhyme with chips. One class in a 4+ unit came up with *hips and chips* and *whips and chips* which were then inserted into the poem.

Teachers who have the confidence to rap can also reinforce the rhyme and the rhythm by rapping a story. *Rockpool Rap* (Roderick Hunt) from the Oxford Reading Tree Series is a good one to start with, although it does need practice! One adventurous student teacher, Karen, rapped *Noah Built an Ark One Day* by Colin and Jacqui Hawkins and went on to do a series of lessons based on the book. A more detailed account of this student's work with a Reception class follows.

A case study

1. The objectives for the sessions were to:
   - listen attentively to a story
   - demonstrate a recognition of the rhyming words
   - share an enthusiastic response to the text
   - interact with the text by active involvement
   - demonstrate an awareness of a grapheme/phoneme connection
   - show an awareness of how texts are constructed
   - have fun.

2. Karen chose the book *Noah Built an Ark One Day* because:
   - it is a simple repetitive story
   - it uses alliteration and rhyme
   - it follows a progressive sequence
   - the illustrations are layered and amusing and a good resource for questions
   - the story of Noah was familiar to the children.

The first session

Karen began by slowly tapping out a consistent beat and repeating 'it's raining' until the children became silent and listened. The development of routines, especially if rhyme and rhythm can be incorporated, is useful, not least for capturing the children's attention and this is an activity in which the children can join.

Next the book was 'read' as a rap, placing emphasis on the repetition and rhyme. Then the story was repeated, omitting the rhyming words. Quite spontaneously the children provided them. As the story was being read the children began to beat out the rhythm, but observed by the student were children who were 'out of sync' with the others in the class. A mental note was made of those children who required further rhythmic activities. One child read the story to the rest of the class who helped him to recall the rhymes in the story.

It is perhaps worth while to consider the assessment indicators of this first session. They were for the children to:

- sit quietly and listen attentively
- volunteer rhyming words
- demonstrate ability to beat out a rhythm
- recall a sequence of events.

In the evaluation Karen noted the four children who had been unable to 'hold' the rhythm. Otherwise this had been a highly successful session.

The second session

This happened in the afternoon when the younger children went home. The aim was for the children to internalise the story by sharing a response to the text, with the student building on the listening and participatory skills from Session 1. The story was 'read' again and the children were asked questions, such as:

- Why do you think Noah took the animals on his ark?
- What do you think the animals did all day aboard the ark?
- Tell me more about Noah.
- What do we know about doggy?

Drawings were made on sheets which had rhyming couplets from the story and children were encouraged to read these. It was while discussing the text again that ideas and concepts were drawn out of the text. Concepts were discussed such as kindness, rudeness, and cooperation: 'Noah was kind because he rescued the animals and the pig was rude for calling the hippo "fat".' The drawing task also allowed for the teacher to interact with individual children. Finally the book was looked at again in order to consider some of the conventions of print through questions such as 'Who is the author/illustrator?' 'Where do you begin to read a book?'

The third session

The aim of this session was to extend the young readers by active involvement with the text through performing the story of Noah. The children read their 'lines' from the sheets containing the rhyming couplets they had drawn on earlier, even 'rapping' their own lines. They swapped over sheets to play different roles and in some cases the children adopted different voices for different characters.

In conclusion

This was obviously a valuable learning experience for the student as well as for the children. Although Karen's work was part of an assignment on reading, speaking and listening played a key role in these sessions. As well as learning about rhyme and rhythm, performing, discussing issues, and learning the 'rules' of discussion, the children experienced the sheer pleasure and joy of playing with the language. The learning took place through talk which was a vehicle for learning about literacy, while the children were also learning about talk itself.

Other authors/titles

Alan Durant	*Mouse Party.*
Colin and Jacqui Hawkins	*Mr Bear's Aeroplane.*
Margaret Mahy	*When the King Rides By.*
Rosemary Wells	*Noisy Nora.*
Storychest Series	*Smarty Pants.*

Listening

Often in a busy classroom, what we mean by listening is children listening to our instructions and carrying them out promptly. Of course this kind of listening is significant, yet listening is also part of the interactive nature of talk. Activities to improve children's listening skills, sometimes produced to complement a reading scheme, might ask children to detect one sound from another. Their value needs to be considered carefully. Are they testing hearing or memory only? Listening corners are being developed now in classrooms to include a tape recorder and a selection of tapes of stories or songs for the children to listen to. The importance of these is that they encourage children to interact and are based on children using their imagination in listening. They also provide different models of listening which move beyond the purely instructional listening that can become the exclusive mode in the busy classroom. We need to put children in situations in which they are invited to listen and respond. Role play is one such situation.

Role play

This is a complex form of play and is sometimes referred to as 'fantasy play' or 'socio-dramatic play' in which children pretend to be Mummy, Little Red Riding Hood or Doctor, with the house or home area being the usual context in which role play takes place.

Free play

Free-flow fantasy play, important as it is, does not necessarily engage the children with each other or lead to the development of language. Children are often left to play on their own and this is important. Often in their play they will be Mummy or Daddy yet they are not just imitating adults – they are, in these pretend situations, preparing for and rehearsing real life. The teacher will have set up the shop or café in the house with the help of the children, but the pretend game is theirs; they have ownership and the leeway to initiate a situation.

In one Reception class Abida, Razia and Joanne were playing in the house. They had taken saris from the dressing-up box and helped each other on with them before going into the kitchen part of the house. They discussed what they were going to cook, talking together in Panjabi, at the same time repeating what they were saying in English so that Joanne would understand what they were going to do. They proceeded to make chapatis using the actions of mixing and patting of the dough they had observed at home. They then pretended to fill a pan with water and, after putting it on the stove, they 'filled' the pan with what they decided was rice. During this activity they talked together about what they were doing, moving from Panjabi to English and back as they discussed with Joanne what they were doing.

This activity is an example of the way in which observing and noting children's free play can provide us with important information about the cognitive, linguistic and social skills which children are manifesting and developing in their play. The cooking represented for Abida and her friends an important link between the worlds of home and school, enabling the children to develop skills in school which they had practised and observed at home. This helps to give relevance to their learning in school. The children with English as an additional language, in moving from Panjabi to English and back for the sake of their English friend, were providing important evidence not only of their linguistic skills as bilingual learners, but also of their ability to use the appropriate language on the appropriate occasions. These children were certainly showing a knowledge of what language is about.

The important lesson here is: don't ignore play; observe it and look for opportunities to develop it and the talk arising from it. Children's play can convey information about their knowledge and understanding of the world around them. Yet we also need to ensure the children are engaged in contexts which require them to communicate and collaborate. Self-maintaining statements such as 'I'm going to be the baby now' do not constitute the interactive talk which is required in role taking. Adult intervention in play can provide an environment in which children have the opportunity to collaborate and interact with a more experienced language user. This can be achieved by observing the children's play and looking for opportunities to join them and develop what they are doing.

Adult intervention

We might next revisit the class shop and recall its value in imaginative play. The area has been turned over to a shop, with posters around proclaiming bargains or advertising the best brand to buy. Some of these have been begged from a local store, some have been made by the teacher and others by the children. The money is in a pretend cash till which is flanked by a table containing empty packets of food, plastic bottles, pots of creamy desserts, etc. One child is behind the table being the shopkeeper and another is arriving at the shop, carrier bag over one arm, while helping along her 'baby' with the other. This scene is a common one in many early years classrooms.

The children will have been playing in the class shop for several days. The teacher will want to extend the activity and relate their play to their real-life experience of shopping in order to give them the opportunity to find the words to give their experiences meaning. The teacher can provide a starting point for taking the talk further by asking the children about their real-life shopping. She might ask them what they are buying, where they are going, who they are going with, what they do when they return home. On the other hand, the teacher might want to intervene directly in their play and there are several ways in which she can do that:

- Will the adult enter the shop and ask for directions to the Post Office?

- Will she introduce a time limit to customers – this shop is closing in five minutes?

- Will she pose a problem – 'What can I have for tea tonight?' 'What can I make with what I have bought?'

The adult needs to think about how she can enrich and deepen the play, to engage the children in a variety of talk and yet not to take over the shop! This will require sensitivity and forethought in order to provide what Neelands (cited in Moyles 1994: 97) calls the 'subtle tongue' of the teacher. This last point is worth considering further. Do we have a *laissez-faire* approach in the classroom or a didactic one? I do not believe it is a case of either/or, for both of these methods have their value and teachers recognise this.

However, there is an additional approach to teaching and learning grounded in the teacher looking for, and taking advantage of, opportunities to intervene in the child's activities – not to instruct, but to collaborate with the child in order to facilitate their learning. In this way, the educator needs to be on hand in order to assist the child and help reinforce understanding. The teacher needs to recognise the 'teachable moment' in order to intervene (Woods and Jeffrey 1996). It is worth noting that in the Primary National Strategy's handbook, *Speaking, Listening, Learning: Working with Children in Key Stages 1 and 2* (QCA/DfES 2003: 23), it states that in order to ensure progression in speaking and listening teachers 'should help children to extend and sustain their talk, for example by joining in the interaction'.

The difficulty, given the limited time for observation and listening teachers have at their disposal, is having the relevant information about what the child already knows and thereby engaging in a conversation that helps the child to develop their knowledge further. In order to provide opportunities for these kinds of conversations, finding ways of helping children to become more independent in their learning environment can enable the teacher to give more time to observing and listening and to recognise and take advantage of the 'teachable moment'. There is of course no one answer to this difficulty and every teacher has a different solution. One might usefully examine the classroom environment. Does it assist the child to become independent? Are teachers or their assistants too ready to jump in and do things for the child? For example, do the children know where all the equipment is or do they have to ask the teacher each time where to find a resource?

Activity

What other situations can you think of and what kinds of intervention can you plan? You could begin with the ongoing activities in many classrooms, such as sand and water play, block play or sharing a book.

Language diversity

Although this is a complex area for young children it is an aspect which we can begin to talk about in the early years. Raising awareness of the different ways the children talk is a starting point. Ask children:

■ How do you greet your friends/head teacher?

■ Do you speak differently to babies/grandparents?

■ Do you have different words for going to bed/feeling tired?

■ Do you have different words for kinds of food, e.g. sweets/lolly/toffees?

Reading stories and poems containing a variety of speech also helps to raise awareness of diversity, although some aspects of this last point perhaps need to be considered. Can or should we affect another dialect or accent? Teachers fortunate enough to have a varied language background can easily take on accents or a dialect from their own repertoire, for example the Yorkshire tones of *Stanley Bagshaw* by Bob Wilson, but how desirable is it to adopt another accent when reading perhaps the Anansi stories?

Completing a language profile is a useful activity and promotes a great deal of talk about talk and the language we use. To begin with, it is worth while for the teacher to complete her own language history, using the following questions:

■ Where were you born and how has that affected the way you speak?

■ Have you moved and has that altered the way you speak?

■ How has your education affected the way you speak?

■ Does your accent reflect your social class?

■ Do you vary your accent at all?

■ Do you speak in a regional dialect, standard English, a patois, and do you vary your dialect according to the person you are talking to?

- Do you have another language that affects when and where you speak English?

- Does the way you speak reflect your age?

- Could you change the way you speak, and why?

These questions are taken from eastLINC materials (Smith *et al*. 1991).

An easy and enjoyable way to present your own language repertoire to children is to bring in a photograph of yourself as a child and tell them the story of your language.

Other authors/titles

John Agard	*I Din Do Nuttin'*. Poems.
John Agard and Grace Nichols	*No Hickory, No Dickory, No Dock.*
Allen Ahlberg	*Burglar Bill.*
Tony Bradman	*Adventure on Skull Island.*
Dick King-Smith	*George Speaks.*
Kaye Umansky	*The Fwog Pwince.*

Conclusion

This chapter ends with the words of a four-year-old, Linda, who was part of my research. This transcript of a conversation with her mother as she is being put to bed shows Linda is able to use talk in a highly sophisticated way.

Linda:	I like you best.
Mother:	You like me best?
Linda:	Not when you shout at me.
Mother:	Not when I shouts at you? (*laughs*) You should be good shouldn't you? Eh? 'Cos if you was a good girl sometime I wouldn't have to shout at you would I?
Linda:	You don't like shouting?
Mother:	No, I don't like shouting at you and I don't like you being naughty.
Linda:	Don't you? Don't you think it's a shame when I cry?
Mother:	Do I think it's a shame when you cry? Sometimes.
Linda:	Sometimes you don't?
Mother:	Yes, sometimes I don't, 'cos sometimes you get sent to bed don't you?
Linda:	When I get sent to bed don't you care?
Mother:	Of course I care. Do you care?
Linda:	Care about you.
Mother:	You care about me?
Linda:	Every day.
Mother:	Every day?
Linda:	Even when I'm being naughty.

By their first day at school most children have learned how to talk and many of them, like Linda, in a very sophisticated way. That enormous development children have made in the first four or five years of their lives can now be given range, diversity and depth through systematic teaching in the early years classroom.

Further reading

Tassoni, P. and Hucker, K. (2000) 'Providing opportunities for language and literacy', in *Planning Play and the Early Years*. Oxford: Heinemann.

Whitehead, M. (2002) *Developing Language and Literacy with Young Children*. London: Paul Chapman Publishing.

Listening to Children's Talk: Oral Language on the Playground and in the Classroom

Elizabeth Grugeon

Chapter 2 has shown the importance of the home and community where children have already become competent speakers and listeners and where, as well as their unique family narratives, they have had access to a variety of media materials: TV, film, video, music, computer games, mobile phones and other aspects of digital technology (Hall *et al.* 2003). They share a cultural landscape and communicative practices outside school from which they will have drawn 'textual toys': media materials, songs, narratives, characters and images (Dyson 2003). These unofficial media materials will soon become part of their official school concerns and are part of their developing literacy practices where, through a process of recon-textualising, they will intricately weave their textual toys into official school contexts (Dyson 2003: 15–17).

This chapter looks at children's informal language on the playground and at their developing skills as storytellers in the classroom. It is based on work on the playground and in the classroom where trainee teachers, acting as researchers, listened closely to children's talk. As a researcher you take on a very different role to that of teacher; the relationship between teacher and taught has shifted. You do not know the answers and your questions have to be genuinely investigative, closer to the kind of questioning recommended by Robin Alexander (Introduction, p. 8) and the resulting talk will be nearer to the dialogic model proposed in *Speaking, Listening, Learning* (QCA/DfES 2003). By observing children's spontaneous play, listening and recording it, we can learn about interests and obsessions which may not surface in the classroom. Teachers need 'to be aware of both their pupils' passions and preoccupations and how these can be productive in enabling new meanings to be created' (Millard 2003: 7).

Playground observation

We can observe how drama and role play occupy the children, how playing with language fascinates them and how they draw upon a repertoire of traditional games and the popular culture that surrounds them outside the classroom. On the one hand, they may be playing games like British Bulldog and Red Rover, or chanting counting-out rhymes that their parents knew; on the other, playing at Pokemon or Harry Potter and games based on Gameboy and PlayStation. The discourse and language of the latter can be complex; the games fast moving, collaborative and confident. In her research, Dyson describes how 'for many children media materials provided textual toys that permeated the unofficial world and that could be drawn on for participation in the official one' (2003: 76) and how 'the children used textual toys, for pleasure, performance and dramatic, often collaborative play' (139). Careful observation of their play can inform ways in which teachers can draw these into the formal, official curriculum.

Recording and explaining children's talk on the playground

Students at De Montfort University, Bedford, were required to record interviews with children playing informally on the playground. Looking at their transcripts tells us how and why the children were playing these games; it reveals how much they make media narratives their own. Media texts are a relatively recent phenomenon: insofar as they are multimodal, a child may encounter Harry Potter, for instance, through one of the books, the films, CD-ROM, audio tape, packets of sweets, T-shirts, a trading card game, a Game Boy version, models, a website. 'Each story exists in a veritable cosmos of texts all revolving round a core fiction' (Mackey 2002: 31). Some children may first meet Harry on the playground in the games their friends are playing; others will have encountered the merchandise rather than the book or film. Mackey sees this as perfectly normal for the children of today; she describes the way children use a range of tactics to create a textual world that is meaningful to themselves. She suggests that there are different ways of responding to the enormity of the technological and commercial options now pressing for our attention. She feels that in a wildly confusing textual world, the young have a great deal to teach adults about the 'art of selective and autonomous attention' (Mackey 2002: 38). Playground games would seem to be one way in which they are doing this.

Marsh and Millard (2000: 45) suggest that, 'Because contemporary children's play is often bound up with popular cultural icons which are unfamiliar to many adults, suspicion is cast as to its inherent value'. But if teachers of young children are prepared to recognise what children already know and can do, what Dyson calls their 'cultural resources' (2003: 5), and acknowledge that this will include their considerable exposure to media and popular culture outside school, it can be used positively in the classroom. As *Curriculum Guidance for the Foundation Stage* states:

> Young children's learning is not compartmentalised. They learn when they make connections between experiences and ideas that are related to any aspects of life in the school setting, at home and in the community.

> (DfEE/QCA 2000: 45)

Popular culture inside and outside the classroom

It would seem developmentally appropriate to capitalise on the wealth of language and literacy displayed on the playground, and to use the children's interest in and understanding of popular culture and their creative involvement in role play to bring this into the classroom as a basis for teaching literacy (Grugeon and Harding 2004).

There is much argument for the inclusion of popular culture in the primary school curriculum to enhance learning and motivation (Gee 2003; Kress 2003; Lambirth 2003; Marsh 2003; Millard 2003; Dyson 1997).

Defining literacy

Looking at what children are playing has helped student researchers to take part in the wider debate about dominant literacy practices within school; to consider the existence of multiple literacies and the need to look beyond the focus on print literacy which dominates their training. Lambirth (2003: 11) suggests that 'Working with a unitary model of literacy, as contemporary curricula do, arguably creates a danger that will inevitably, implicitly ignore other literacy practices that occur in homes, working places and other social settings away from the school'. He has found that teachers are generally wary about the inclusion of popular culture texts in their teaching, despite the very strong arguments for more appropriate forms of literacy for the education of children in the twenty-first century (Kress 2003). Gee (2003: 14) argues that literacy, 'even as traditionally conceived to involve only print, is not a unitary thing but a multiple matter...there are different literacies'. The evidence that the trainees collected from the children on the playground gave them insight into the pervasive influence of new technologies in their pupils' lives and the extent of their engagement with popular culture. Analysis of their data has acted as a springboard for their own understanding of the need to address the 'multiliteracies' that are needed to function in the modern, media-saturated world. They will be prepared to consider Millard's notion of a 'transformative pedagogy' which proposes a model of literacy that effectively fuses children's cultural interests with school requirements. This 'literacy of fusion', Millard (2003: 7) argues,

> relies heavily on a teacher's attentiveness to the interests and skills brought into the classroom and their skill in helping children transform what they already know into stuff that will give them agency in a wider world and allow them to become more critical of their own and others' 'meanings'.

Understanding children's interests outside the classroom

The trainee teachers' independent research gives them a starting point; they have been particularly attentive to children's interests. Their careful interviews show how creatively children interpret media texts and take ownership of them. They have seen how children subvert media messages and mock the texts they are using, and they recognise that the youngsters are hardly the passive recipients that adults often fear. They have also become increasingly aware of ways in which teachers are effectively cutting themselves off from significant aspects of children's everyday lives by constantly banning media-based crazes, toys and games from school playgrounds. By the end of their research they can see that there is a powerful argument for welcoming these. The activities the trainees have observed and recorded are both multimodal and intertextual, ranging across media forms – visual, audiovisual and verbal. They are a reflection of the 'integrated marketing' that characterises children's contemporary media culture. The trainees involved in playground research are hopefully better prepared to take on this challenge armed with their personal knowledge.

What the children have to tell us

Reading the transcripts of the playground interviews and the pupils' thoughtful comments can tell us a lot about the way children use considerable linguistic and imaginative skills to transform the influences they are receiving outside the classroom.

Activity

Look at the transcript below and consider what this tells you about the players' knowledge and skills. The extract comes from an interview with two boys. They are playing *Toy Story*. One child is Woody, the other is Buzz. A student researcher asks 'How do you play the game *Toy Story*?'

Child 1:	Well, it's like the PlayStation game...we just go around and we get the coins and Pizza Hut tokens...
Student:	Where are the Pizza Hut tokens and coins?
Child 1:	Well they're...
Child 2:	They're around. You know, like over there (*points to the corner of the playground*)...Well, that's the toy cupboard, and then there is the bedroom...
Child 1:	Over there, that's the garden. Sometimes we can't get the coins because there's baddies there...
Student:	How do you decide who is who?
Child 1:	We just *say*. I am always Woody, the Cowboy. Sometimes we fight and he wins because he has more things than I do...you know, he has a laser and he is a space ranger and has wings and a helmet that opens when you press the button...
Student:	What do you have?
Child 1:	Nothing much...sometimes a horse, but not much...
Student:	Can you stop the baddies?
Child 1:	Sometimes. Buzz can get them with the laser and I can get them with my rope. I swing it round (*demonstrates*) and then it wraps round them and they can't move...Can I go now?

You might consider the following points:

- Look at the student's questions. What does she want to know and why?
- Look at the children's answers. What does she learn from them?
- What sort of props are they using?
- How would you describe the way they are playing this game?

Discussion

- Because the interviewer is evidently mystified by the boys' first answer she has to ask searching open questions that will allow the children to answer at length.
- The children set the scene for the drama they are enacting and show how they imaginatively locate the different settings in precise areas of the playground.
- The props exist in their imaginations.
- They have adapted and transformed a game that they play on the screen. They have created a narrative which they enact with complete conviction, imagining the lassoo, the laser gun, the retractable helmet and the different settings for the drama.

Comment

Many students recorded similar instances of children absorbing and adapting characters and stories from the videos and computer games they are familiar with into their fantasy play. They were able to comment on the language the children were using. For example, much swapping and bartering was observed: two Year 6 boys trading cards involved a confident use of the language of the Pokemon universe:

Child A: I'm not giving you that for only one Squirtle. It's not worth it. He's only got three power points to Charmander's five. No way, nah... what else?

Child B: That's stupid, 'cos Rychu can have up to seven blast power points if you put him with Squirtle... yeah?

Child A: No way, it takes too long for them to evolve... I'm not giving that.

Another of the students, Linda, saw a wider range of activities and much evidence of the influence of TV, film and computer games. She lists these as:

Mario, based on a TV and computer character, which involved weapons with prescribed effects. Players call out: Thunderbolt, Green Shell, Yellow Star, and other players know powers and how to respond. Star Wars Episode 1 Racer which involved rushing round in 'pod racers'. There was a weapon, the 'flame jet' but so powerful that no one was allowed to have it. Pokemon Blue was a chasing game played by a mixed group, running in a circle, sitting on the ground and chanting 'Pokemon, Pokemon, Pokemon Garadoss'. Pokemon cards were largely out of fashion, but trading of Pokemon Game Boy games, done by linking machines together, was very popular indeed.

She was assured that Game Boy machines were allowed in school as long as teachers did not see them! Computer games that they were familiar with, such as alien games (Quake Tree Arena), action games (Indiana Jones) and cartoon games (Yoshi), were also influencing the games they played.

Using props for dramatic narratives

In an urban lower school, Lucy described the way children used collectable soft toys in their play. She watched three Year 2 girls:

> One had Mystic, the unicorn Beanie Baby, and for most of the game it hung out of her pocket while the following activity was carried out. All three girls leapt out of the school door and wove their way around the playground, flapping their arms. I later found out that these were their wings. They finally met up in a grassy area of the playground, well away from the school buildings. They gathered leaves, twigs and grass from the nature area and arranged them in little piles.

In conversation with Lucy, they described how they were making little nests; this was clearly an intertextual reference to *The Lion, the Witch and the Wardrobe* ('Our teacher read us the bit about the fawn who lived in the forest') and also to Bambi – they were all familiar with the Disney video.

Imaginative recreation

Children are not simply responding to these texts or events in a passive way. Looking at what the students have recorded shows the extent to which children from 4 to 11 years old creatively absorb these into their play culture, exploring themes and issues that they make their own through imaginative narratives. Looking at what the children tell the students shows the extent to which these games, far from deadening their imagination, feed and extend possibilities for new narratives and new language development in their pretend play.

Clare interviewed three Year 4 boys:

Child 1:	Well, we get our ideas from Card Captors and Pokemon…me and Jacob had the idea of using transporters, like little machines, walking transfers…
Child 2:	Transport us in the worlds
Child 1:	Bringing the future into the world of dragons and back into the present – into our normal world
Child 3:	And magical world
Clare:	What is it called?
All:	Dragon Cards

Listening to them, Clare realised that these 'cards' are entirely imaginary: 'They go on to describe how they fire arrows through the cards which unleash the dragons and allow them to battle with them'. She feels that they have drawn upon a range of media influences here:

> Card games such as Pokemon and Card Captors have inspired Child 1 to come up with a game that has similarities to those games mentioned but with his own imaginative input. They have produced imaginary cards of dragons with varying powers. The three children all know what the different

cards are and what they do without having to actually see them. They have given the dragon cards names, such as 'Ghost Dragon', 'Thunder Dragon' and 'Ice Dragon'. These represent the elements and what the children might class as dangerous things. The idea of magical worlds comes from their different media experiences; the words they use clearly reflect these. Included in their game is a city called 'Diagon City' which has been taken from Harry Potter. Another of their interests was the TV programme *Dungeons and Dragons*. Their game includes weapons, guardians and creatures of power.

The children continued to talk to Clare:

Clare:	Do you have any accessories, bits you need to play the game?
Child 1:	Well, we need the cards
Child 2:	The stick that we use to fly on and we use to shoot the animals. Child 1 (*sic*) and me and Jacob and John have just started a story
Child 3:	The Fairy Dragon
Child 1:	No, the Ice Dragon – our first ever card is the Fairy Dragon and our second card is the Ghost Dragon
Clare:	Do you buy the cards?
Child 1:	No, we pretend we have them
Clare:	Oh, do you make them up?
All:	Yes
Child 1:	We find them – we can't capture the champion levels, what are Ice Dragon, Fire Dragon or Lightning Dragon, because they are more powerful than any card. So we have made up cards – mine's the Ghost Card
Child 3:	Mine's the Demon Card
Clare:	Do you have those? Do you draw them out or do you pretend you've got them?
Child 1:	We pretend we've got them

Looking at the transcript of this long discussion, the imaginative involvement of these three boys in their game is impressive.

Clare:	And you made the whole thing up yourselves?
Child 3:	Yep, with a few ideas from other things

The powerful use of pretence

This heightened involvement is illustrated by many other examples the students have collected and which they frequently comment on. Natasha writes:

Most prevalent on the playground were 'pretend' games. They varied between those that used stories and characters obviously derived from popular media and those that involved more of the children's own imaginative construction. The children were extremely keen and able to describe the narratives of their games; they appeared to be very intense. There were many games that were directly based on stories or themes taken from the media, such as Harry Potter, Buffy the Vampire Slayer, Blind Date and Pop Idol.

She observed boys absorbed in playing with James Bond cards: 'These are collected from magazines, and play involves voluntary exchanging and play for cards based upon strength and weapons described in each character's profile. The game leads to discussions about characters and there is a great deal of competition about who knows more about the cards and also the films. I found that boys would draw designs for computer games based on the cards.

Narratives and play with language on the playground

This spontaneous storytelling on the playground is a strength that teachers can build on in the classroom. Also the spontaneous role play and mini-dramas which constitute the main part of the games observed must suggest ways of harnessing this enthusiasm. Carla, like many others, witnessed the role playing of the very popular TV programme *Pop Idol*:

I interviewed a group of Year 4 girls who were carrying out a singing contest, imitating the structure and content of *Pop Idol*. The girls take on roles of the TV personalities and pop stars. They demonstrated a clear understanding of the rules and structure of the game, allowing each contestant to sing a song while the 'judges' sensitively listened and gave support.

On another playground, Sonia observed the judges being less supportive:

Based on the talent-spotting television show, girls re-enacted the audition, selection and rejection process of the contest. As in the show, the judges were portrayed with certain personality traits. On one occasion, I witnessed a 'judge' criticising a 'contestant' with a continuous series of derogatory comments. Interestingly, these were all in the form of similes such as 'your voice sounds like a strangled baboon' and 'your hair is like the straw on a scarecrow's head'. As this was expected of the judge in question, the remarks were taken in good part and contestants were expected to react accordingly by either leaving the 'stage' in tears or stomping off.

Sonia noticed how the girls were enjoying playing with language in this way, vying with each other to find alternative ways to describe performances: 'incredible', 'unique', 'outstanding'.

Again you will notice how the children delight in playing with the sounds and meaning of words outside the classroom.

Play in the early years

Louise, who was working with much younger children in Reception and Year 1, felt that the examples of vigorous and imaginative play she was recording were shaped by the children's familiarity with video and television, particularly *Buffy the Vampire Slayer* and *Power Rangers*. The children had told her that they watched these on Cartoon Network. She had heard a lively discussion in the classroom about 'transformers' and a 'super hero robot' and had noticed that children brought these toys to use on the playground. She writes, 'The youngest boy in the class was very interested in "Super Hero" and this was often reflected in his animated conversation, drawing and emergent writing and "small world" play in the sand.' She considers the fact that adults may question the suitability of the wide range of video and TV programmes that young children are watching, but feels that there are positive advantages to be gained: 'Many storylines of fantasy games can be compared to the genre of more traditional tales of heroes and monsters and good triumphing over bad'. In their play she had observed children using a range of complicated dialogue and 'alien' vocabulary demanding careful pronunciation.

> Young children's memory and acute attention to detail amaze me when it comes to their verbal and pictorial description of favourite characters in programmes and films. All these emerging skills are a result of engaging with a media form that excites interest and fires the imagination of the children. They identify with and become their 'super heroes' and, although play may often appear rough, it is important as an adult to look more closely at the level of speaking and listening involved, the storytelling, organisation of events, development of character and intrinsic understanding of plot.

Playground interaction and cooperation

Students who have been engaged in this research recognise that the playground is a site for creative, cooperative drama where the children's inner passions and obsessions, drawing on their access to popular culture, are played out day after day, playtime after playtime, enabling children's imaginative life to gain full expression. The child and his or her peers are the key creators and performers, recreating essential dramas and emphasising the excitement of sharing narrative structures to explore fundamental emotions. In the next part of this chapter we look at students working to link this enthusiasm to a more structured way of dealing with narrative and storytelling in the classroom.

Developing children's oral language through storytelling

The confident way we have seen the children using language on the playground, using versions of the narratives they encounter in the world outside school, suggests that there is a rich resource to be drawn on and developed. The stories that children hear before they enter school have been shown to have a profound effect on their language and literacy development. Chapter 2 has illustrated and emphasised the importance of building on the language experience that children bring into school from their family and community and has suggested that much of this is in the form of stories that have been told and read to them. A study of stories told by pre-school children illustrates the power and importance of these resources: the 'narrative techniques that they have absorbed from their experiences of hearing written language' and the syntax that is necessary for complex thinking (Fox 1993: 116). The structures of the stories that they hear, and often retell, help them to anticipate the way stories work as they learn to read. Hearing stories read to them and sharing books with adults has been shown to be the best predictor of children's subsequent experience of learning to read (Wells 1987). However, we cannot assume that this experience is evenly distributed across the population; we cannot assume that all children will be able to transfer home learning to the school setting and be able to tell stories or cope with narrative structures easily and spontaneously. Research carried out over a year in a nursery classroom has shown the sensitive skill and understanding used by the teacher as she involved the class in narrative 'to such effect that by the summer months they are capable of sustained and coherent retellings of stories they have heard' (Dombey 1992: 2). In the process, Dombey describes how they learn a number of complex lessons about narrative which are relevant to their future as readers.

Required to tell stories

A major outcome of the NOP in 30 local education authorities (LEAs) from 1989 to 1993 was the emergence and documentation of storytelling as a significant factor in the development of oral language across the primary age range. The promotion of storytelling at this time has left a legacy of good practice (Howe and Johnson 1992; Grainger 1997; Grugeon and Gardner 2000; Harrett 2004) which has made a significant contribution to the English National Curriculum Orders. The first requirement at Key Stage 1 Speaking and Listening, 'Breadth of Study', is that the range of activities should include: 'telling stories, both real and imagined' (8a). 'Knowledge, Skills and Understanding' require pupils to 'speak with clear diction and appropriate intonation; choose words with precision; organise what they say; focus on main points; include relevant detail and take into account the needs of their listeners' (DfEE/QCA 1999: 16). All these are skills which will be developed by oral storytelling and the NLS framework reinforces this. Text level work from Reception through to Year 6 includes oral storytelling: in Reception and Year 1 the emphasis is on developing understanding of story structure; stories may be re-enacted through role play and using puppets; oral retelling will develop understanding of sequence, character, dialogue and features of story language. In Year 2, role play and individual retelling will continue to develop this understanding which will become increasingly important to the development of pupils' written work. In *Developing Early Writing* (NLS 2001: 9) oral telling and retelling 'where they are helped to say it like the book' are seen as important ways in which children come to understand the features of written texts. In Year 3 an increasing familiarity with a range of traditional stories will allow more sophisticated discussion of typical story themes, characters and language; retelling will continue to make an important contribution to a more explicit understanding of narrative texts. By Year 5 'preparation for oral storytelling' sees this as a presentational skill in its own right (DfEE 1998c). This is also a skill that teachers need.

Storytelling and literacy

The Literacy Hour requires teachers to model the skills they are teaching and to become confident storytellers themselves. This chapter shows how teachers developed this competence working alongside their pupils. The more recent teaching objectives (QCA/DfES 2003) track storytelling through from Years 1 to 6, linking this to NLS objectives. This starts with 'tell stories from their own experience' and 'retell stories' in Year 1; in Year 2, 'to tell real and imagined stories using the familiar conventions of story language'; in Year 3, 'to prepare stories for performance'; in Year 4, 'to tell a story using voice effectively'; and in Year 5, 'use notes to cue techniques'. The Drama objectives also draw on storytelling: in Year 1, exploring stories using improvisation and role play 'to act out own and well-known stories'; in Year 2, 'to present traditional stories [and] own stories'; and in Year 3, 'to use drama strategies to explore stories' (QCA/DfES 2003: 12–18). Storytelling continues to be seen as a very significant feature in the development of speaking and listening.

Reflecting on storytelling in school

We will look at the way a group of teachers in training came to recognise the different resources that children already had, and how they responded to them and developed them. These accounts reflect their own, as well as the children's, growing understanding of ways in which narrative may help children to make sense of a wide range of experiences while providing evidence of their developing competence in speaking and listening. In the edited transcript below, two trainee teachers talk about their experience of sharing stories with the children in their Reception and Year 1/2 classes.

Jan: ... they were receptive to storytelling at any time of the day...

Val: We'd find that they were always willing to come and listen to a story and it was our main form of communication ... if you brought them onto the carpet, telling a story, you were as one, sharing excitement, thrills, sadness, happiness, many emotions.

Jan: Yes, and many of the stories would spark them off and they would leap up wanting to tell you a story, something similar that had happened at home ... 'Oh that's what happened to me', would come the cry and they would leap up one after another, trying desperately to tell you their own stories, which was a very exciting experience.

Val: And they found leads in our stories and went off and did other very creative things, they wanted to illustrate the stories ...

Jan: I told the treacle one, about the monkey...

Val: Who gets, 'only trouble'?

Jan: I told that and many other African stories and the children would look at the words – *How the Lion Roars* described the sound the lion made – and the children were looking at whether the words described the meaning, they looked at the language ...

Val: I was a bit worried about the monkey story, thinking my children were a bit young for it. I was concerned they wouldn't understand the African words but the children really enjoyed it and understood every word of it, though they did ask a lot of clarifying questions such as 'Why did he choose a prickly tree?' They asked a lot of questions to put it straight in their minds, but they enjoyed it.

Jan: But did you find they were able to retell the story straight away or the major incidents? I mean, there were children in my class who were able to tell back the story throughout the day. They were telling children in the class ...

Val: Ah, that was something else, the storytelling corner I set up, I had two tape recorders, one with blank tapes and one with tapes to be listened to. This corner was used every minute of the day…the children were so prolific with their stories.

Discussion

As you read this extract from a much longer discussion:

■ What did you think the students were discovering about storytelling in an early years classroom?

■ What do we learn about their strategies as teachers?

■ What contribution might these storytelling activities make to the children's literacy development?

Comment

The students were evidently surprised by the powerful effect of story on these young children; they discovered that storytelling was

■ a means of communication and control;

■ a means of sharing experience;

■ a stimulus for other activities;

■ a stimulus for looking closely at language;

■ a means of developing expertise as tellers and retellers;

■ a means for questioning and discussing issues.

At the same time they were extending their own repertoire as tellers, trying out a range of stories and providing resources for the children to listen and tell for themselves.

We can see how they are beginning to identify the different resources that children already have and consider how they can respond to them.

Becoming storytellers: a case study

The examples we are going to look at are taken from written assignments by student teachers. They were required to prepare stories to tell during a four-week school experience and to use this experience to write an assignment. As they account for the strategies that they used they are also developing and making explicit the theoretical knowledge and understanding that will underpin their language and literacy teaching in future. The students were specialising in English on a Primary BEd degree. Their written assignment asked them to account for and analyse the outcomes of the storytelling that they had undertaken. They were not only expected to become storytellers themselves, to introduce and develop this skill with the children they were teaching, but they were also to develop a theory that would support a critical analysis of the work they had been doing. They had spent some time discussing and practising appropriate stories before they went into school but they all felt nervous about the prospect of oral storytelling. They all recorded their initial misgivings about storytelling. One of the problems they all faced was the lack of models to follow. The status of storytelling in some schools was fairly low and few of them had experienced examples of teachers telling stories to any but the youngest children. It was not uncommon for students to report, 'Many of the teachers I had worked with did not even read stories'. Negotiating for time to do justice to work they had prepared was often problematic, 'It was difficult to make oral storytelling an important part of the curriculum because my teacher believed the proper time for stories was the last session in the afternoon which lasted for ten minutes'. You may find that this continues to be a problem; National Curriculum requirements have brought about tighter timetabling of the primary school day. This makes it harder to introduce approaches like storytelling if they are not part of the overall plan for a particular class. You may have encountered professional storytellers in school or had the opportunity to attend local events which included storytelling. However, despite support from the National Curriculum, the National Literacy Strategy and the National Primary Strategy for the inclusion of storytelling and encouragement to develop children's awareness of narrative techniques at Key Stages 1 and 2, it still tends to be a rare activity, especially with older children. Storytelling at Key Stage 2 is no less important than at an earlier stage, yet may be less in evidence.

Developing confidence as storytellers

Students found that it was easier to introduce storytelling in early years classes where there has long been a tradition of oral storytelling with young children (Colwell 1991). However, they were soon to discover that telling rather than reading is a particular skill and that once the printed word is abandoned the text becomes negotiable with the audience. As one student discovered:

> My first attempt at storytelling was *The Three Little Pigs*, because I know the story so well. As soon as I said, 'the wolf ate up the first little pig', the children were visibly upset, so I said, 'but he didn't, he went to the house of the second little pig'.

Moreover, the choice of story itself may have to be negotiated. Another student completed her carefully prepared version of *Little Dog Turpie* only to find that the class wanted to tell her about a local event that she was unaware of, 'Five days previously the chimney of the power station a few miles away had been blown up, the largest explosion in England for 20 years'. Most of the children had seen this event on local television and the student gave up *Little Dog Turpie* for their dramatic demolition stories.

The difference between telling and reading

Once students had got over their initial nervousness about telling a story they were able to reflect on their delivery and the children's response. One wrote,

> Two differences which are immediately noticeable are the freeing of hands and eye contact.
> …Freedom from the book facilitates increased eye contact enabling the teller and listeners alike to

share the experience more directly. This close contact with the listeners enables the storyteller to gauge their reaction to the story more accurately, to pick out children who seem worried about the story and those that are not giving it their full attention. Freedom from the text allows the storyteller to deviate when needed to give a fuller explanation when something seems puzzling. ...Best of all, oral storytelling allows the teller and the listeners to create the story afresh each time.

Preparing to tell a story

Students reflected on the need for preparation: 'The most important criterion for choosing a story is do you enjoy the story yourself, as to prepare the story for telling you will have to become saturated in it'.

Before they went into school for a block of teaching, the students had an experience of being in the audience themselves. A local teacher, who was a professional storyteller, came into one of their sessions to introduce them to Anansi the trickster spider (Haley 1972) from the Caribbean. She talked about the importance of telling traditional tales and building up a personal repertoire of tales from different cultures. As well as making them aware of the potential for using props, magnetic and felt boards, puppets and artefacts relating to the story, she had reminded them how such stories can be a way of exploring real-life dilemmas; how they can 'transcend and unite cultures by depicting universal morals and truths' (Gregory 1996: 116).

The students had also joined a group of children at a dramatic telling of *The Hairy Toe* (Summerfield 1970) by one of the university's drama lecturers. Both sessions had helped to prepare them for their own storytelling; as one wrote, the first session had made them aware of the importance of 'having at one's fingertips a range of folk tales from many cultures to use in today's multi-ethnic classrooms in order to broaden everyone's horizons'. The second session had provoked thoughts about the way a potentially frightening story might be handled, or mediated, by the teller. One of the students described how she felt that this had happened:

> Firstly, the way the story was told, the 'virtual' nature of the language and the voice, committed the children's minds and senses and, secondly, the emotion of fear was kept at bay by inviting them to become involved as participants and partners in the telling.

Telling and retelling: the children take over

Becoming storytellers themselves was only the first stage of the process. The next stage was to enable the children to tell stories and for the students to analyse these stories. All were surprised by the quality of the stories told by children. Sue recalled that 'it was the most unlikely people who displayed the most unsuspected linguistic resources and strategies'. A quiet boy who 'would often just nod in response to the register and never participated in class discussion' one day whispered to her that he had a story to tell and began, 'once upon a time in a country not far from Milton Keynes lived a little kitten called Tootsy', revealing a hitherto hidden ability to organise language and tell an elaborate story.

Sue taped the stories told by her class of 28 five- and six-year-olds. She had begun by telling short anecdotes about her pets, hoping that the children would respond with similar stories from their experience. She had expected simple stories but was surprised by the complexity of the narratives that they embarked on. Listening to the recordings that she had made, she was able to trace complex threads linking stories and observe how children seemed to be grappling with issues that bothered them. She comments on two stories told by Kerry:

Kerry:	There was a dog and its name was Punk and it went outside and keeped on barking, and it was one of them big ones.
Susanna:	Dalmatian.
Kerry:	Dalmatian, and it...
Susanna:	Spotty dog?
Kerry:	No, one of them ones with black and gingery colour.
Student:	An Alsatian?
Kerry:	Yeah, and it keeped on barking at everybody. All the little children keeped on getting scared 'cause it was that big. He had to go home and he got smacked and if he went near the food he will have no dinner for a hundred years... I can't think... or go to the vets and get killed.
Student:	Oh gosh!

Sue commented, 'My final reaction shows that I was not expecting Kerry to end her story in this way. It was obviously, however, her way of coming to terms with what was uppermost in her mind. Her story had been a safe way of allowing her views to emerge. I saw Kerry still trying to resolve the obvious conflict in her mind when a week later she told me the following story about an incredibly 'good dog':

Kerry:	A little dog what was good, and it was nice and kind and it was trained good and it gived people their food and it got the letters and it stayed on its own and it keeped on cleaning up everywhere and it was a nice dog and they said 'we're going out for a walk with you' and they took it for a walk and there was a big puddle – about that big...

Reflecting on these two versions, Sue felt that Kerry was trying to sort out a dilemma about good and bad behaviour, about crime and punishment. She felt that the stories were helping Kerry to develop her own views of the world and that, 'as Betty Rosen says, the story allows her views to "emerge safely"'. Moreover, it emerges with the help of her audience, Susanna, who is evidently listening intently, anticipating and predicting outcomes.

Teller and audience

The importance of an audience, the social nature of storytelling, was remarked on by several of the students. Some children seemed to have an amazing command of technique. Jane writes about a seven-year-old:

His tale was fascinating, the story of a little boy who finds himself, having gone through a small door in a cave, entering a quite different world on the other side, a world of monsters. It was apparent that he was using visual clues to help provide details; for example, 'there was a monster school with monster chairs' (looking at the chairs) 'and monster music' (looking at the music stands). It was equally apparent that he was transforming what he actually saw into some kind of visual imagery, and that he could transmit such images to his audience. An interesting aspect of Toby's story was the monster teacher who spoke monster speak and whom the little boy could not understand. I asked whether the boy ever managed to understand, to which Toby replied 'No, never'. I was left to wonder whether there was an implicit message in this story. Bruner (1986: 64) says that 'the young child seems not only to negotiate sense in his exchanges with others but to carry the problems raised by such ambiguities back into the privacy of his own monologues'. Toby's command of devices to convey meanings and atmosphere and his grasp of the conventions of story grammar were impressive for a child of seven years. Perhaps the most linguistically mature aspect was the ending – 'It had all been a dream'.

Intertextuality

All the students had found evidence in the children's stories of their reference to stories that they had heard and read before. They were discovering that 'any story presupposes the existence of other stories . . . for both reader and listener threads of connection exist, threads of many different kinds' (Rosen 1984: 33). Most of the stories recorded bore out Carol Fox's finding, in her own study, that 'The model for the children's stories was very obviously literary' (Fox 1993: 97). Kerry's stories drew on two stories that Sue had told the class. The monster story that Jane refers to has many intertextual references. Many of the children chose to retell familiar fairy tales. Wendy recorded a story told by a four-year-old as he was drawing a picture:

John:	Now the elephant is on the ground.
	Now he's changed to green
	And when he was on the ground he changed to green.
	When the chameleon is on the floor it changed to green
	When it's on the floor this chameleon
	When, when the elephant is on the floor
	it changes.
	Mrs Smith, when the elephant is on the floor it changes green like a chameleon.
Donna:	No, it doesn't!
John:	It does 'cos it's a magic elephant.
	There is the chimney and the smoke is coming out
	And it's nearly going to fall on the elephant,
	A changing elephant and when it's on the floor it
	changes yellow.
Donna:	Oh!
John:	I don't know what this is going to change into . . .

While this monologue might not seem to be a story, John seems to be developing a narrative structure. Wendy, who knew where it was coming from, felt that it was most certainly a story: 'John has created an elaborate story around the previous week's tale of *The Mixed Up*

Chameleon (Carle 1988), the drama of the chimneys and this week's folk tale of *The Elephant and the Rabbit* about an elephant who changes his appearance'. In combining real and fantasy events, Wendy felt that he had begun to create a 'possible world' into which Donna was beginning to be drawn.

Children learning to tell stories

Peter Hollindale (1997: 70) reasserts what has become a generally held belief when he claims that

> we construct our selfhood through memory; that we depend for our identity on our sense of personal continuity in time, and that we express this to ourselves by storying our lives . . . we need stories as we need food, and we need stories most of all in childhood as we need food then, in order to grow.

However, such an assertion naturalises narrative and storytelling, and can lead to a belief that there is little for teachers to do other than provide the appropriate stimulus and context, and the children will tell stories confidently, drawing on some pre-existing resource. As it was, this group of students found that they needed to work very hard with children who did not find telling stories easy. Jane reflected on children in her class who had needed help and drew on her reading of Jerome Bruner and Gordon Wells to help explain why this might be the case:

> I noticed that he managed the opening and the beginning of the sequence very well but he became confused about how to describe his actual holiday experiences. In fact, this is no easy task since the capacity to construct stories from experience requires, a 'natural organisation of mind, one into which we grow through experience rather than one we achieve through learning' (Bruner 1986: 63).

Her reading of Gordon Wells' *The Meaning Makers* (1987) offered her a plausible explanation for another child's difficulty in constructing a sequence of events from memory. Wells suggests that, 'making sense of an experience is to a very great extent being able to construct a plausible story about it' (Wells 1987: 196). Jane wondered whether the child was unable to construct a story because she could not make sense of her experience or vice versa. She reflected that in either case the child would need plenty of talking and reflecting to help her, 'through conscious exploration of memory, to internalise the meaning of her experiences'.

Reflecting on the experience of storytelling

By the end of their four-week school experience students had begun to account for an impressive range of skills and versatility in the repertoire of young children as they created, reshaped and interpreted their experience. They had discovered latent oral narrative skills, both their own and the children's, which they were able to analyse, becoming aware of ways in which a storyteller, in unique ways, is thinking through language. They had also found that narrative was not as easy for children as they had supposed and needed careful planning, intervention and support. Their research and analysis had been supported by their reading. They had found Bruner (1986) and Wells (1987) particularly helpful. Carol Fox's early articles had helped them to recognise ways in which storytelling was helping their pupils to shape experience and develop narrative strategies. They were providing evidence from themselves to support Fox's study (1993) which concluded that the model for young children's story-telling is predominantly literary. The pre-school children in her study seemed to use the genre of fantasy stories rather than personal experience since these 'probably lend themselves to a greater degree of elaborating than narrating a real-life experience' (Fox 1993: 97). The students, however, had noticed that their slightly older children were combining both these elements, confidently using the rhetorical devices of the fairy tale and fiction stories that they were hearing in school and combining these with their own real-life experience.

Other influences on the children's developing oracy such as peer interaction on the playground, the shared experience of TV, video and computer games were also becoming evident. By the end of the four-week teaching experience they were all able to draw on the theory they had been reading to analyse the evidence that they had collected and as a group produced a convincing argument for the structured development of children's oral language through storytelling. The importance of narrative in the early development of literacy should not be underestimated:

> Children who engage in the business of building narratives in their heads are extending the arena of their meaning-making to include worlds far wider than the world of the here and now. These worlds are also more ordered, more linguistically self-contained and perhaps more amenable to inspection, than are those created out of the flux of first-hand experience.
>
> (Dombey 1992: 1)

In a chapter entitled 'Playing the Storyteller: Some Principles for Learning Literacy in the Early Years of Schooling' (Hall *et al.* 2003) Carol Fox argues for a much greater awareness of the diverse literacy skills and experience that children possess when they enter the classroom:

> We need to develop a better understanding of the knowledge of distinct discourse styles and structures that children bring with them to school from the outside world, to see how spoken and written channels overlap and interflow in those discourses, and to recognise how linguistic knowledge of this kind can be used to make literate transformations from speech to reading and writing and back again. One way to discover this kind of discourse knowledge would be to place oral storytelling and role-play close to the centre of the early years curriculum.
>
> (Fox 2003: 196)

This chapter has focused on some of the ways in which we can find evidence in our own classrooms to support this assertion.

Further reading

Dyson, A. H. (2003) *The Brothers and Sisters Learn to Write: Popular Literacies in Childhood and School Cultures*. New York: Teachers College Press.
Grainger, T. (1997) *Traditional Storytelling in the Primary Classroom*. Leamington Spa: Scholastic.
Marsh, J. and Millard, E. (2003) *Literacy and Popular Culture in the Classroom*. Reading: NCLL.
Rosen, B. (1988) *And None of It was Nonsense*. London: Mary Glasgow Publications.

Developing Articulate Readers

Lyn Dawes with Sandra Birrell

Spoken language is children's most powerful tool for formulating and expressing their thoughts. Talk offers children an immediate, flexible medium with which they can have an impact on those around them. They learn to use this tool – to become articulate – by speaking and listening with others. Articulate children are in a strong position. They have the means to do such useful things as question, describe, persuade, inform and speculate. They can use this facility to help themselves understand the social and physical world around them. More than this, they can encourage others to talk to them, giving them a better chance that their fluency in spoken language will make exponential gains. As the literate child learns to read and write while learning from reading and writing, the articulate child make leaps of understanding and development while becoming better able to use spoken language effectively. Conversely, children limited by lack of vocabulary, lack of confidence or poor language awareness may well become frustrated by their inability to communicate. Of course there are other ways children can express their feelings and ideas – for example, a smile, a punch or a hug – and eventually most are able to write down what they want to say. But talk remains the best and most accessible way for the majority of children to open up their thoughts, to interact with other people, and to learn. This remains the case as we grow into adults. Although much exchange of ideas goes on through writing and reading, people in all areas of their personal and working life organise meetings, discussions, one-to-ones, conferences, talks, phone calls, dinner parties, and get-togethers of various kinds where much gets learned, clarified and decided through talk. Education must offer children ways to become articulate as an investment in their future; but just as importantly, so that they can make the most of their present.

Speaking and listening for literacy

So that we can make this happen in schools, the National Literacy Strategy (NLS) (DfEE 1998c) encouraged the use of spoken language in whole-class and group work but did not specify the direct teaching of speaking and listening as a discrete subject. The QCA guidance materials *Speaking, Listening, Learning* (QCA/DfES 2003) addressed this omission by providing a framework to support the development of the skills and understanding children need to become articulate. The approach depends on the fostering of children's progress through activities with specified learning objectives for speaking, listening, group work and drama. The child working through these activities can be expected to gain an awareness of the importance of their own 'voice', to develop appropriate vocabulary and spoken language tools, and the confidence to use them purposefully.

> An articulate classroom is a community of learners and teachers who share an understanding about the roles of talk in their learning and the many social contexts they experience. Oracy, like literacy, will both be part of every subject area and a subject in its own right.
>
> (Goodwin 2001: xv)

Dialogic teaching

In Autumn 2003, a group of Year 4 students undertaking De Montfort University's BEd course were asked to use their understanding of the importance of spoken language to evaluate their own talk with children. The students were enrolled on an English course in which much attention was paid to the teaching of speaking and listening. Weekly seminars were used by the tutor to model dialogic teaching (Alexander 2003). Dialogic teaching is based on the premise that learning in schools is a social activity. Social aspects of classroom contexts which teachers can organise to help ensure the effectiveness of learning activities are:

- the fostering of a classroom community in which learning dialogues take place;
- the creation of activities which necessitate learning dialogues.

Learning dialogues are conversations in which challenging questions feature strongly. An open and inquisitive attitude is essential to learning dialogues. In learning dialogues different points of view are seen as a positive resource. Children are aware that through speaking and listening they are thinking together, and that focused talk is necessary to help everyone develop their ideas. In classrooms, learning dialogues are based on explicit learning objectives so that the children know what they are doing, why they are doing it, and how to achieve their objectives through discussion.

The BEd course aimed to generate raised awareness of the importance of talk for thinking and learning, and to provide practical strategies for implementing a talk-focused approach in practice. The students completed a school-based task in which they read and discussed a suitable book with a small group of children from their class. The students transcribed their discussion and analysed the interaction to highlight points at which it was possible to 'see' learning taking place. This chapter includes a contribution from one of these students, Sandra Birrell. She recorded her talk with a group of children and this conversation is used later in this chapter to illustrate how a teacher with a particular awareness of the importance of talk can guide and support children into deeper understanding of a specific book – and help them take crucial steps towards becoming literate and articulate. The children's names have been altered to ensure anonymity.

The guided reading group

Sandra shared the picture book *Where the Wild Things Are* (1963) by Maurice Sendak with three Year 1 children, recording the conversation and transcribing this in full. Since the school did not commonly conduct guided reading sessions, the children had little previous experience of discussing their ideas about a book in depth. Sandra selected Anna, Dawn and Jack as competent and willing talkers who were among the most able readers in the class. Anna was 6:1 at the time of the task. She had a reading age of 7:7 at 5:9, based on Salford Reading Test (SRT). Dawn was 6:1 at the time of the task. She had a reading age of 5:9 at 5:9 (SRT). Jack was 5:11 at the time of the task. He had a reading age of 6:5 at 5:7 (SRT). In order to maximise the opportunity to generate collaborative talk, Sandra began by looking at *Come away from the water, Shirley* (Burningham 1977).

Picture books, with their detailed illustrations and motivating narrative structure, are open to a range of interpretations and can provide a terrific stimulus to help teachers to generate talk and thinking. Each child will bring their own ideas to their understanding of text and graphics. If encouraged to share such ideas, they gain the opportunity to consider other points of view, to reflect and learn. This sort of thinking together aloud is invaluable preparation for thinking alone.

OFSTED's (1995) finding that it was taking too much time for teachers to listen to children read individually led to the formulation of 'guided reading'. With many variations in format, guided reading sessions generally involve children organised in ability groups reading individual copies of the same book. By listening or joining in with the group talk the teacher can gain insight into levels of individual reading competence and comprehension. During guided reading, the NLS says, 'Challenge may be in terms of reading cues and strategies, language and vocabulary, or sophisticated aspects of grammar, inference, skimming and scanning' (DfEE 1998c: 80). Considering the role of talk, the NLS sets out the format of guided reading sessions: 'the teacher discusses the text with the pupils, drawing attention to successful strategies and focusing on comprehension' (DfEE 1998c: 81). This is a good example of how learning is expected to proceed through the medium of talk; though until 2003 the teaching of speaking and listening for learning was given little direct attention by the NLS.

Guided reading as a social way of thinking and learning

Discussion of the text under study is an integral part of guided reading. The purpose of such discussion is to ensure that individual children attend to and comprehend the details of what they see and hear. Each child in a guided reading group can be expected to interpret the text slightly differently. However, the overall learning gains will depend not only on the child's previous experiences, but on the text, the illustrations, the group and the task as organised by the teacher. In addition, and most profoundly for young readers, learning depends on the chance to hear the text read, repeated, analysed and commented on, to share ideas about the pictures and the story, and to ask and answer questions. Guided reading is in essence a very social activity. The child joins a mini-learning community for the duration of the session, in which the discourse creates a fertile habitat for developing as a reader. It is an unusual situation; parents or librarians may read to children, classmates may occasionally share a text, but very rarely will the child be part of this sort of 'book club' setting. The talk focus is of great importance for getting the most out of the text and one another.

Learning to read is not a linear process; it proceeds in leaps and small incremental steps at different times. The ultimate aim of teaching reading is to help children develop into independent readers. Guided reading offers learners the support of both classmates and teacher. A real advantage is that children in guided reading groups can tackle books that they would fail to read alone. They can gain satisfaction and confidence from this achievement, as well as acquiring skills and understanding about both the book and the process of reading.

The NLS has encouraged teachers to organise *shared* reading, writing or speaking and listening, involving whole-class work. It is based on learning intentions decided in advance by the teacher. Children work in teacher-led sessions on a range of tasks. *Guided* reading, writing or speaking and listening tends to happen in groups which may or may not be asked to work collaboratively. Each individual will construct different meaning from these guided sessions. Peer support is offered, as are other structures such as ICT-based 'speaking books', writing frames, or ground rules to enable effective group talk. *Independent* reading, writing or speaking and listening is, at best, personally motivated. The child has an aim for the 'work' which may transcend the achievement of learning objectives. For example, a fluent reader may take her book home to finish reading it; a child may type a chatty email to a friend; a child may ask a classmate what he thinks of a film they have both seen.

The teaching of literacy is driven by educational learning objectives, and by the child's personal impulse and purpose. Guided reading, writing and speaking and listening provide special contexts for learners. In these situations, learners move away from imposed expectations towards making use of literacy for their own purposes. Paradoxically, use of group work is a strong support for independence. In addition, guided groups offer increased skills, knowledge and understanding of literate practices generally.

Guided reading as exploratory talk

Whatever the format of guided reading, it should include an element of exploratory talk (Mercer 1995; and Chapter 6 of this book), which is essentially a particular type of dialogue in which partners engage critically but constructively with each other's ideas. The concept of exploratory talk is derived from the work of Barnes (Barnes and Sheeran 1992: 126) who says, 'Exploratory talk is often hesitant and incomplete; it enables the speaker to try ideas, to hear how they sound, to see what others make of them, to arrange information and ideas into different patterns'.

Dialogic teaching of guided reading involves the teacher knowing where the discussion might lead. The teacher takes the responsibility for upholding the discussion, and in so doing allows the children to bring their ideas forward for the attention of others. Talking to children about books involves asking questions which may be thought-provoking, interesting, or downright impossible to answer. Sometimes, it is in not knowing that new learning lies. Not only that, the teacher also has to encourage readers to raise their own questions – genuine queries which they really want answered. Teachers model this 'probing' by raising genuinely-interested questions themselves. This involves not only knowing the book under study extremely well, but in wanting to know what the children think, and in being prepared to learn more about the book from them. This sounds a lot to ask; but teachers commonly achieve this small miracle of teaching-and-learning, using knowledge while remaining open to new ideas. It is simply an area of professional expertise.

An example of effective guided reading

In the next section, Sandra analyses her guided reading discussion, highlighting some key issues for teaching and learning. Sandra's contribution is included as an extended quotation.

Considering their lack of experience, I thought the children coped well with the two talk activities and showed great enthusiasm. I shared the objective for the discussion of Burningham's book: 'We are learning to talk about a book and read text and pictures to help us understand the story'. I told the children I hoped they might have some questions to ask and some comments to make, so that we might have a chat about the book and help each other to understand it, adding that we might not find out the answers to our questions. I noted that Jack spoke the most and Dawn was the quietest.

Subsequently, I recorded our talk about Where the Wild Things Are. *I was generally pleased with the discussion and believe that I can show evidence of learning taking place. I took 153 turns in the conversation, while Jack took 99, Anna 71 and Dawn 56 turns. Many of my turns were questions, because I believe that asking probing questions helps children to see how to generate such questions themselves.*

I tried to ask questions to which I really didn't know the answer. Some of these questions scaffolded the children's thinking and learning, for example by asking for evidence, *e.g. 'How do you know he's asleep?'*

Sandra:	You think it's just a dream?
Jack:	'Cos he's asleep.
Sandra:	How do you know he's asleep?
Jack:	'Cos he's going like this.
Anna:	Yeh. And he's got his eyes closed.

or asking for clarification, *e.g. 'What makes you say that, Jack?'*

Sandra:	He scared them?
Anna:	Yep.
Jack:	But why would he scare them? – they, they could just, kill him.
Anna:	Yeh.
Sandra:	What makes you say that, Jack?
Jack:	'Cos of sharp claws.

Another example of asking clarification is, 'But you're sort of saying you don't think this would be true, really, are you?'

Dawn:	I know why they're scared of him – 'cos they think, erm, he's a monster, too, and he's stronger than them.
Sandra:	Right. They think he's a monster? Maybe. He's different to them, isn't he? – so, he's something they don't know about. But you're sort of saying you don't think this would be true, really, are you?
Jack:	No, I don't . . .
Sandra:	Because he's a little boy in a wolf suit and they're big monsters.
Jack:	Yeh.

I used my contributions to show respect for the children's opinions:

Jack:	He'll go back home.
Sandra:	You think he'll go back home?
Dawn:	Yeh.
Anna:	But he is in his home.
Sandra:	Right. That's interesting. He is in his home.
Jack:	Yeh, but he goes back home in his dream.
Sandra:	Why did you say that, Anna?
Anna:	Because at the beginning, then there's like his wall and the trees.

I repeated or reformulated many of the comments made by the children, sometimes in question form, and tried to encourage them to extend their thinking, e.g. 'That's one of the monsters, Jack's noticed. So what do you think that means? Does that tell you anything?' The talk shows that all three children brought some of their own experience to the book. Anna mentioned Jesus as an example of a king who is not bossy. This comment came while the children were talking about the monsters crowning Max king:

Anna:	Yeh, but he's, he looks a bit bossy.
Sandra:	You think he looks bossy?
Dawn:	Yeh. But it's just a dream.
Sandra:	Do you think a king would be bossy?
Jack:	Erm, yeh.
Anna:	But Jesus isn't, and he's a king.
Sandra:	Right.
Dawn:	Yeh, but Jesus ain't . . .
Sandra:	Not every king's the same.

Other examples of children contributing ideas based on previous experience or knowledge are when Dawn talked about the moon: 'The moon is bigger than this planet, ain't it?' (though her understanding of the solar system could be the subject of another discussion!) and Jack introduced a monster he'd already heard about: 'I liked it when he meeted that monster – the Loch Ness monster'.

The discussion helped the children to reflect on their own ideas, and to shift their opinions with a fluidity created by confidence in the supportive nature of the talk. Initially Dawn was persistent in her opinion that Max was dreaming, using this word five times. She then changed her mind and told us seven times that Max was thinking, *even contradicting Jack: 'No. He hasn't got a dream. He's thinking'. All were quite happy to express their own views and to change their minds. Anna disagreed with Dawn that the 'wild thing' on the cover could be a dinosaur, but later suggested this herself: 'They're dinosaurs? Monsters?' She also contradicted me: when I pointed to a picture and said, 'The sea looks rough, doesn't it?' she replied, 'No it doesn't'. Anna reminded us twice that Max did not really leave home because the jungle appeared in his room, and yet, she thought he had been somewhere when we were talking about his supper still being hot, because he was out of the room when his parents brought the meal. Jack had his own opinion about when the dream started, but I believe he was influenced by Dawn's idea that Max was thinking, concluding, 'He's thinking like daydreaming'.*

Jack seemed to get most involved in the text, laughing quite a lot and making more spontaneous comments about things he noticed, e.g., 'They still look the same but Max doesn't. 'Cos he used to not have a crown' and 'Hey, he's got human feet!' Jack was the only one to ask questions: 'Why's he hammering that thing on his wall?' and 'But why would he scare them? – they could just kill him'. He also makes a prediction that Max will jump out of the window and puts himself in Max's shoes by saying, 'What I would do is, erm, get a golden gun and shoot them in one shot so that they die'. As Fry (1985: 99) says, 'Our picturing as we read puts us there in the story, and unless we find ourselves there, the story passes us by'. I think Jack did find himself there.

In the following sequence, the children understand what Anna means well before I do, and patiently offer me help:

Anna:	Sometimes it's hard to read without because it's like *w*, it's all together.
Sandra:	Sorry. Say that again, Anna.
Dawn:	But this one's just a dream.
Anna:	It's sometimes hard to write with, read without because sometimes it's all together.
Sandra:	It's hard to read without what, Anna?
Jack:	A space.
Anna:	Without spaces in without.
Dawn:	And without full stops.
Sandra:	Oh, it's hard to read the word 'without', because it hasn't got spaces. I see.

Guided reading provides good opportunities to discuss unfamiliar words. In the following sequence, the group considers the word 'rumpus'. Jack uses the pictures to suggest this means some sort of parade, with Anna thinking that people might bow and curtsey to whoever is parading; and that the monsters are jumping. Dawn suggests 'party time'. Later Jack notes that the monsters are shouting. The group is sidetracked into talking about the moon, so that the definition of a rumpus never really becomes clarified and none of the children subsequently uses the word in their talk, suggesting that they are not fully confident about its meaning. However, the guided conversation about this book has served to introduce a new word in a meaningful context – a useful first step towards eventual understanding. The word rumpus has become helpfully associated with party, shouting, parade. When asked to say which part of the story she enjoyed most, Dawn says, 'I liked the bit where the monsters and the boy was having fun.' I ask, 'Where they were having the rumpus?' to which she agrees. She thinks that having a rumpus is some sort of fun; the Collins English Dictionary *defines rumpus as 'disturbance, noise, confusion' – which any parent will recognise as a children's party!*

Sandra:	. . . 'let the wild rumpus start!' (*pause*) What do you think a wild rumpus is?
Anna:	Erm, it's . . .
Jack:	A parade or something.
Sandra:	A what? – sorry, Jack.
Jack:	A parade or something.
Sandra:	A parade?
Jack:	Or something.
Anna:	Or maybe, you would like (*mimes*)
Sandra:	Bow? – bow and curtsey? Maybe. Let's have a look. So here we haven't got words. We've only got pictures, here.
Dawn:	Party time.

Anna:	Yes.
Sandra:	So this is the rumpus. What do they seem to be doing?
Anna:	Er, jumping, and maybe it's just like a little parade.
Jack:	Looking at the moon.
Sandra:	Looking at the moon, yes. It's a full moon, isn't it? – that's what we call that, when it's, we can see all of it.
Anna:	A parade.
Sandra:	It is a bit like a parade, isn't it? Yeh.
Dawn:	Do you know what? The moon is bigger than this planet, ain't it?
Sandra:	They seem to be... They've got their arms up in the air as though they're, sort of, bowing down, aren't they? And what's Max doing?
Jack:	Shouting.
Anna:	It's just a piece of rock in the sky – that's what the moon is. Now they're swinging on trees.
Sandra:	Swinging on trees?
Jack:	Yeh.
Sandra:	Is the moon still there?
All children:	No.
Anna:	Because it's the morning, or afternoon.
Sandra:	Oh it's the morning now? So they had the rumpus all night long, then.

The crucial importance of teacher guidance

I really believe that the children helped each other understand the book through this discussion. My influence was to provide structure, direction, support, encouragement, clarification, questions and to be an active listener. I had not prepared any questions in advance, but I knew what sort of discussion I would like the children to experience. I concluded that the discussion helped the group to interact meaningfully with a fiction text, learning from one another about the book and providing the children with insights which could inform their reading of other books. I think that guided reading encourages children to look at books thoughtfully, using inference and imagination to involve themselves in the story. In guided reading settings the child's emotional response to the story – their delight, surprise, interest and curiosity, for example – can be communicated to others. Enjoying books is infectious and a good discussion generates enjoyment. I think that frequent opportunities to engage in discussion of texts, such as the one I recorded, are very valuable, for all the reasons given above, and because they not only teach children about reading but about speaking and listening as well.

Activity

Tape record one of your own guided reading sessions. Listen to and analyse your tape. Consider the children's contributions, and your own, in the way Sandra illustrates.

- Can you pinpoint evidence of thinking together and developing ideas?
- How can children be encouraged to ask one another more questions?
- What could you do to enhance the children's experience of guided reading?

Further points from the guided reading transcript

Sandra's guided reading session was a rich experience for this group of children. The discussion lasted about 20 minutes; during this time the children were fully engaged with one another and the text. We can see that, knowing they are safe to do so, they offer ideas, respond to questions and share their amusement and interest. Sandra asks the sort of questions that will facilitate talk: 'can you say...?' 'do you think...?' 'what does that tell you...?' and says explicitly, 'that's interesting...' We can see learning taking place. In the transcript extract below we can see how the group probes the idea of dreaming/thinking/daydreaming, and how Sandra's use of the word 'daydreaming' is picked up or appropriated by the children. In the following sequence they extend their vocabulary, their ideas and their confidence. We can see their thinking in the talk.

Sandra:	He's feeling fed up. Yeh. He's had his bit of adventure. He wants to go home.
Jack:	They want to eat him.
Anna:	But he is in his home!
Sandra:	They say they want to eat him, now. And you're saying he still is in his home.
Jack:	Yeh. He still is, but in his dream he wants to go home.
Sandra:	Right. So off he goes.
Dawn:	No. He hasn't got a dream. He's thinking.
Jack:	Yeh, the thinking I mean.
Sandra:	When you say that, Dawn, do you mean that you don't think he's asleep?
Dawn:	Yeh.
Sandra:	That he's still awake but he's sitting there daydreaming? Is that what you mean?
Jack:	Yeh.
Dawn:	Yeh.
Anna:	Yeh.
Dawn:	I think he's thinking.
Sandra:	Right.
Jack:	He's thinking like daydreaming.
Anna:	I think he's just daydreaming.

This dialogue is very satisfying to read, and must have been very satisfying to be part of. The children were given access to a wonderful book by a skilled teacher whose understanding of the crucial importance of discussion enabled them to learn through exploratory talk.

The discussion highlights some important issues for teachers. All the children appeared to be 'thinking aloud' and were able to support or expand on each other's ideas. They had imaginative, interesting answers to Sandra's 'why?' questions. However, they did not ask one another for opinions; in addition, they offered their ideas without ever saying 'because' or making their reasoning explicit. Having identified this problem, it can be addressed. Learning to give and ask for reasons is an important next step for these young readers. The advantage of guided reading is that such sessions enable children to hear what other people think, because of the presence of the teacher not just as guide through the text but as a discourse guide, prompting and supporting effective talk. The children may learn how to conduct this kind of discussion by taking part in guided reading. In addition the direct teaching of talk skills through talk lessons (see Chapter 6) can help children to understand the importance of their talk with one another, and provide them with clear skills and strategies for questioning and reasoning.

Four important worries about guided reading raised by teachers

1. *It may be very difficult to work intensively with a small group for a reasonable length of time.* Teachers are very creative in organising their own time and that of teaching assistants and other helpers. A weekly guided reading session is an invaluable learning experience which makes all the organisation worth while. A class of children can learn that everyone will have the opportunity to participate, and understand the importance of avoiding interfering while guided reading takes place. Their own enjoyment of the experience may help them to recognise the importance of letting others immerse themselves in a learning conversation about a book.

2. *Some children want to read at their own pace and seem averse to sharing books through discussion.* For some children, the 'stop-start' pace of guided reading can seem frustrating. Understandably, they just want to get to the end of the story and find out what happens! There is a case for reading the book straight through first, so that some of the narrative tension is lessened, and indeed so that the book can be enjoyed simply at this level. Interrogation of pictures and text can then take place to try to work out, for example, why it seemed so exciting, and if everyone had the same first impressions or had noticed the same things. Learning to consider things carefully is useful in itself, as is learning that your ideas might not be the same as everyone else's.

3. *Children rarely raise questions themselves, but are very passive and expect the teacher to do all the 'work' of the conversation.* When children do not raise questions, this may be because they have become accustomed to waiting for someone else to do so. Teachers raise lots of questions, for example during introductory and plenary sessions; if the teacher is part of a talk group, the child may assume that the teacher will take on the task of questioning. There are probably lots of ways round this, one of which is simply to raise children's awareness of this as a problem. Another strategy is to teach children how and why to raise questions; for example, using one storybook page, to talk with a partner to decide on three questions about the pictures, then ask another pair these questions. Non-fiction books are good for this activity too. Learning to ask relevant and interesting questions can be a learning objective for any curriculum-based lesson. For example, in science, given a snail, a woodlouse or a ladybird, how many things do we actually know about the creature? All the things we don't know can be turned into questions. Where does it live? Why is it that colour? Does it live alone or in families? What does it like to eat? Making questioning a habit through teaching questioning as a skill is an important task for the primary teacher.

4. *Teachers question their own role in group discussion, feeling that their intervention is somehow 'wrong' in being too directive.* The role of the teacher in setting up groups, in supporting exploratory talk, and leading the children through the sharing of ideas, is immensely important. It is really inappropriate to worry, as some teachers do, that joining a discussion group is interfering in some way with children's relationship to the text and to one another. While children are learning all the complex skills they need to conduct an exploratory discussion, and to read and interpret text, they need the support and guidance of the teacher. Children can be taught ground rules for thinking together which help them to work independently as groups. Until they have assimilated this way of working they need the teacher to guide the group. Once children can really conduct an exploratory discussion, teacher involvement becomes more a matter of taking part in the discussion rather than orchestrating it.

Conclusion

Teachers who help children to be part of learning dialogues based on a shared book are providing them with key learning opportunities. Speaking and listening can help children to learn to read and write. Guided reading sessions are opportunities for fostering reading skills such as interpreting text, drawing inference, and relating text and pictures – as well as a wonderful chance to enjoy a book together. Guided reading helps children to learn to read and value books, with the added bonus of learning to become articulate speakers and active listeners.

Further reading

Alexander, R. J. (2004) *Towards Dialogic Teaching: Rethinking Classroom Talk*. Cambridge: Dialogos UK Ltd.

Dawes, L. and Sams, C. (2004) *Talk Box: Speaking and Listening Activities for Learning at Key Stage 1*. London: David Fulton Publishers.

Dawes, L., Mercer, N. and Wegerif, R. (2000) *Thinking Together: A programme of activities for developing thinking skills at KS2*. Birmingham: Questions Publishing.

5

Developing Children's Oral Skills at Key Stage 2

Carol Smith

Prologue

Alex:	Mrs Smith, Mrs Smith. I was sick seven times last night and my grandma's gone to Spain.
Hannah:	Mrs Smith, Mrs Smith. My hamster's got conjunctibite us.
Stephen:	Mrs Smith, Mrs Smith. Have you heard the joke about three pieces of string who went into a pub?
Jamie:	Do you believe in all that God stuff, Mrs Smith?
Jessica:	Mrs Smith, how do seedless grapes make more seedless grapes if they haven't got any seeds in?
Danny:	Mrs Smith, Mrs Smith. Is the steam from coffee different from the steam from tea?
Amrit:	Don't you talk them words to me.
David:	You f…… b…. You never listen! I hate you! I f…ing I hate you!
Billy:	Mrs Smith, Mrs Smith. I know a song from Dublin. My uncle taught it me. I want to sing it you.

Most children of this age love to talk and all primary teachers will know that listening to children's discussions, conversations, stories and anecdotes is one of the most rewarding aspects of our job. The informal moments at school when a little gaggle of children gather round the teacher with all manner of stories, happenings and jokes, competing with each other for her attention have more than just a social value. Through the relationships that develop during these friendly talk times, the children grow more comfortable speaking in more formal learning situations, such as the Literacy Hour. Children will talk to each other and to you, the teacher, about everything under the sun, and they need these opportunities to talk. It is all too easy in today's packed curriculum to think that there is no time for talk. I would argue strongly that today, more than ever, children must be given time to talk about their learning and their experiences

I would like to begin with Billy's story. Billy, Billy, Billy. Billy from Glasgow. Billy who was only with us for four terms, but who, in that time, influenced us all and eventually came to terms with his unwillingness to learn. Billy sang haunting Irish folk songs, perfectly in tune. Billy with his whimsical, cheeky humour and his Gaelic football. Billy with one foot three sizes bigger than the other. We miss him still.

He arrived in Alison's class, Year 5, in the middle of term, troubled, belligerent, barely able to make himself understood, barely able to read or write legibly, vulnerable. What did we make of him? What did he make of us? Gradually, quietly, patiently, at break times, lunch times, before school, after school, he began to make connections. He sought us out one by one. During work time, silence, accompanied by disruptive behaviour. Who could he trust? Who would listen to him?

The first breakthrough came through Jim the caretaker, also from Glasgow, also with a family from Ireland, non-judgemental, kind and quiet. Billy became his shadow and so the silent tours to other classrooms began and his confidence and trust grew. He began talking to us. Each teacher would smile and say 'hello', expecting to be ignored but Billy began smiling at us and looking round our classrooms.

The second breakthrough came with his class teacher. He sang to Alison. The first day back after Easter, just after visiting his father and uncles in Dublin. From that song and Alison's tears came a whole repertoire of songs and from the songs came the stories, his stories – part legend, part folk tale mixed with his own real-life story. From the songs and the stories came other locked-away talents. Brilliant mental maths calculations and Gaelic football. He told Katie all about his skills, she played with him one lunch time and then Billy taught everyone in Year 5 how to play this amazing, fast and dangerous game.

The final breakthrough to the unlocking of Billy's ability to learn came when he sang in sharing assembly. His mother came and 350 staff and children watched him. Alone and unaccompanied. Three songs. One extremely rude we were sure.

What Billy's story illustrates is the power of talking and listening in children's learning. Before his learning could develop, he needed to develop confidence in us, his teachers. He needed to trust us and through listening to him we gained that trust. He became a quiet and modest folk hero throughout the school. He had been listened to and had become a respected member of the school community. By building sensitive relationships with staff and individual teachers in the school, his learning was unlocked and he became a joy to teach and desperate to learn.

It is not just a matter of understanding the power of listening and speaking as a tool for learning for children like Billy. Billy's story was unusual. Most children's stories are less dramatic. We need to appreciate the place and value of speaking and listening in the curriculum for all children at Key Stage 2. The teacher's role embraces the development of speaking and listening not just in English and the Literacy Hour but also across the whole curriculum. This chapter is about planning and organising activities to encourage and support speaking and listening in the primary classroom. It will help you find your way around the long-awaited QCA/DfES (2003) materials, *Speaking, Listening, Learning: working with children in Key Stages 1 and 2*. It is also about stimulating powerful learning. Speaking and listening at Key Stage 2 helps children make sense of their learning and helps them come to terms with feelings and relationships.

The aim of this chapter is to:

- explore the reasons why Speaking and Listening is such a powerful element of children's learning in Key Stage 2;
- suggest some practical strategies for making yours a talking classroom;
- give some ways forward when planning for more speaking and listening.

There are several voluntary 'activities' throughout the chapter, which may help you to a wider view of the value of talk at Key Stage 2.

Speaking and Listening – an important element of the curriculum at Key Stage 2

Pupils talk and listen with confidence in an increasing range of contexts. Their talk is adapted to the purpose: developing ideas thoughtfully, describing events and conveying their opinions clearly. In discussion, they listen carefully, making contributions and asking questions that are responsive to others' ideas and views. They use appropriately some of the features of standard English vocabulary and grammar. (QCA 1999)

By the end of Year 6, most children will be expected to achieve this level of competency in Speaking and Listening, one of the three attainment targets in the English National Curriculum for England. Many aspects will be taught through the daily Literacy Hour following the NLS framework of objectives (DfEE 1998c). Teachers and student teachers are coming to terms with the 68 objectives in *Speaking, Listening, Learning* (QCA/DfES 2003) and using them in a creative way in their planning across the curriculum. Almost from the beginning it was realised by teachers that the Literacy Hour could not be taught effectively without good listening and talking skills.

Taking opportunities to use talk in the classroom

Talk in the classroom is crucial to learning. It is where answers to puzzling questions can be found. It is where thoughtful argument and discussion make way for the understanding of new skills and difficult concepts. It is where difficult issues, which emerge from the children's literacy work, their maths or science investigations, history or religious education (RE) studies, can be talked through. It is where children listen to and respect the views of each other and where everyone's learning is empowered by talking about what they have learned. It is where children can be supported in raising their own questions about their learning.

By the time most children reach Year 3, or the beginning of Key Stage 2, they will have come to understand the appropriateness of different kinds of talk in different contexts. By placing a greater emphasis on group discussion and interaction in the *Speaking, Listening, Learning* objectives (QCA/DfES 2003) children should now be given far greater opportunities to talk, discuss and share ideas. How and what they talk about will adapt and change, whether they are in the playground, classroom, speaking in sharing assembly, asking questions of a visitor, speaking to the head teacher, talking in twos, larger groups or just to you or the dinner ladies.

Sometimes, out of frustration, disappointment or anger, children may swear and shout at us, taking out on someone they trust and like their pent-up worries and troubles. By giving children the language of argument and persuasion, we can give them the tools to be more effective and articulate at expressing their views in a democratic way.

Planning for Speaking and Listening in the curriculum at Key Stage 2

All learning, across the whole curriculum, could be said to begin and end with speaking and listening. It would be almost impossible to introduce any new area of learning or revise an old one without some form of questioning or discussion by the teacher and children. Fortunately, in many areas of the current National Curriculum, talk, discussion, explaining, justifying, describing are all prescribed. Talk in the classroom is protected and being actively encouraged. The set of materials which make up *Speaking, Listening, Learning: working with children in Key Stages 1 and 2* (QCA/DfES 2003) are extremely helpful to teachers wishing to ensure they have planned appropriately for the development of their children's skills. The objectives are planned within four key strands: Speaking, Listening, Group discussion and interaction, and Drama, and are across the curriculum. The handbook, teaching objectives and classroom activities booklet, and the posters can be seen as reassurance for the experienced, creative teacher or as starting points for the newer or more reluctant, inexperienced teacher. A good English coordinator will hopefully plan into the school's Continuing Professional Development Programme some opportunities for teachers to work on the Professional Development materials contained in the publication (QCA/DfES 2003). Particularly helpful is the 'Progression' poster, which sets out criteria for assessing progress across the primary age. This will support good planning by encouraging teachers to ask the right questions about their children's development in speaking and listening.

Activity

It may be useful to look at some examples of your most recent short-term planning and identify all those opportunities where children's speaking and listening skills were developed and extended.

Comment

You may also like to reflect on how children's talk skills have improved since the advent of the Literacy and Numeracy Strategies. The structure of Literacy Hours and daily mathematics lessons has enabled children and teachers to engage in a more interactive 'talk' led curriculum. Children need to be able to explain their views, justify choices, methods and decisions.

Fostering talk as a strategy for learning

Arrangements that help schools come to understand and value talk as a strategy for learning include:

- The adoption of a whole-school approach.
- Supportive attitudes in individual teachers, teaching assistants, parents and other children.
- Careful planning and organisation of speaking and listening opportunities.

A whole-school approach is the ideal way to help children understand that what they have to say is valued. It should permeate all areas of school life and include relationships with everyone who works in or visits the school. In most schools, Speaking and Listening has equal status in the literacy scheme of work with Reading and Writing. Indeed, it is the case that plenty of discussion of text is the prerequisite of good reading and writing. In weekly planning it is best to ensure several specifically planned speaking and listening opportunities within literacy and other curriculum areas. These could range from children's word explosions for a poetry stimulus, writing and taping a guided tour of a museum room or favourite collection of Ancient Greek or Egyptian artefacts, to a group reporting the results of a science investigation to the rest of the class.

It is significant that as the NLS develops and supportive documents such as *Grammar for Writing* (NLS 2000b), *Developing Early Writing* (NLS 2001) and, most recently, *Speaking, Listening, Learning* (QCA/DfES 2003) are being widely used in school, the materials actively promote talk at all stages of the writing process. We will now consider what you as a teacher can do to foster talk as a strategy for learning in your classroom

Informal talk time

Overhearing or being part of playground conversations, whether about their school work or about last night's episode of *Neighbours*, *EastEnders* or the result of a Premier League football match, gives us an insight into the way children make sense of events happening in and outside school. A good moan about a teacher who has had to be angry can help dispel feelings of hurt and frustration.

When children talk about their experiences earnestly, it helps them make critical judgements about personalities, events and relationships. Their discussion and analysis help them resolve conflicts with adults, friends, in games and within their own families. We can and should use this insight into the richness of their oral culture to influence our work in the classroom. One junior school head teacher spoke to me recently about the decrease in playground aggression in her school since the introduction of the Literacy Hour. As a result of learning about and using persuasive language and the language of argument, many of the older children were now more able to articulate their responses to disputes rather than resort to physical aggression.

Talking and, of course, listening to others talking helps children take on new perspectives and adapt, refine or even change previously held beliefs or misconceptions. It guides them towards a clearer understanding of the busy and often complicated lives we lead. As in Billy's case, talk takes children towards a positive view of their own opinions and abilities and leads them to a greater sense of self-esteem and respect for the views of others.

The most important thing a teacher can do to help children appreciate the value of talk is to give children time to talk. Not just curriculum time but time at the beginning and end of the school day. Try to be available for a short time at break and lunch times. There is often a reason why children stay behind to 'tidy up', or why a child is last to put his coat on and collect his lunch box at the end of the day. He may need clarification about something discussed during the day:

> Mrs Smith, you know when you said that…?
> Is it really true that…?
> Can I…?

Many clarifications of the children's learning happen at these informal times. Just as importantly as children talking to you about problems in their learning, they may come, in time, to trust you enough to discuss personal and social issues. This is clearly important for all children but becomes increasingly relevant to the older children at Key Stage 2 as they try to make sense of physical, emotional and psychological changes in themselves.

While discussing triangular numbers with a group of Year 6 children, sitting on the carpet, Alan recounted that he would not be at school on Monday because he was going to his grandfather's funeral. There followed a short discussion between the other children, Alan and his teacher about grandparents, funerals and death. Gary's grandma had died in the summer and he had gone to the funeral and told Alan what it was like. Hayley wished she had been to her aunt's funeral but had chosen not to go. The group then continued laying out counters and looking for patterns in triangular numbers. The value of unplanned talk should not be underestimated by the teacher and should be valued as important to school life as a whole. You can plan to take advantage of the unplanned!

Activity

Next time you are on playground duty, or have the opportunity to visit a school playground, take the time to listen to the type of talk the children are engaged in, watch their games, listen to their skipping and clapping rhymes. It might prove much more fruitful and certainly more interesting than sorting out fights and arguments! (Remember to take a notebook and a cup of tea with you!)

Comment

You will probably be surprised at how difficult it was to collect this information. Playground talk is not meant to be overheard by adults. We can only guess at the topics being so earnestly discussed 'under the coats'. During my time as a Year 6 teacher, I observed a group of boys play the same 'Dr Who' game throughout the year with growing sophistication, interchanging roles and leaders of the game. However, when I tried to talk to them about the intricacies of their extended role play, it was clear my enquiries were considered intrusive.

Questioning

When teachers speak to children about their work, asking questions is the most commonly used strategy to assess their learning and progress. We can challenge children's thinking if these questions are 'kept open', leading them into other areas of discussion and further questions. Within the NLS, children are encouraged to raise their own questions relating to text in both shared and guided reading. The best way to support children in developing their ability to respond to open or semi-open questions is to encourage them, early in Key Stage 2 or sooner, to prepare their own questions either for the plenary in the Literacy Hour or for other groups to respond to in guided/independent times. Children also need the opportunity to speak for extended periods of time in order to support the making of connections and sequencing of ideas, and to help expand and consolidate new thoughts and knowledge. A skilled teacher knows when to intervene and further scaffold the child's speaking.

Puzzling questions, primarily used to explore interesting scientific questions, can be a really useful assessment opportunity, encouraging children to think independently or individually in an interesting way and to question their learning. Puzzling questions rarely invite definite answers, more often leading to more puzzling questions. They certainly give children opportunities to discuss their own ideas, particularly in science – 'Why is grass green?' 'Why do we feel pain?' Depending on the context of the questioning, a variety of questioning techniques is to be encouraged.

In order to make learning through speaking and listening more effective, teachers need to give children more time to think before expecting a response. We often expect an immediate answer from children, asking 'reliable' children with their hands up. The quality of response will always be better if time is given for individual thought to a whole range of questions. The use of 'talk partners' in both literacy and numeracy can give children an opportunity to think answers through, sometimes with the aid of a 'whiteboard'. By allowing children plenty of time at first, to think their answers through, you might find they need much less time, as their experience deepens, to discuss and arrive at their answer. Many more hands go up and you can actually 'see' the children thinking. You might even consider stopping 'hands up' altogether, giving a period of thinking time, then specifying who is to answer. Assigning talking partners is really valuable when encouraging less confident speakers, or childen who are new arrivals to your classroom, school or country. Ideas can be shared first with a partner, a teaching assistant or small group; after a little more time, the quieter child will feel able to speak in front of the whole class. Review times during a teaching session help everyone to clarify their thoughts and ideas and frequently spur on those children having difficulty with self-motivation.

Providing the children with an atmosphere of trust in which to talk

Some of the strategies for providing the right atmosphere in which children feel safe to talk have been discussed already in this and preceding chapters. Developing a sensitive and trusting relationship with the children in your class is the most powerful and effective strategy to stimulate talk. However, 'quality' talk cannot be left just to 'happen' in the classroom. Certain conditions have to be in place, since structures and a few rules help to create the ideal atmosphere for speaking and listening. The attitudes and responses of children to each other is crucial and no child should ever be laughed at or humiliated for expressing their opinions or points of view.

'Golden Rules for Speaking and Listening' are best initiated by the children but may need a little guidance from the teacher. One class's 'Golden Rule' is that children should try very hard not to interrupt anyone who is already speaking. A 'Golden Rule' for their teacher is to ask her to select a response from a girl and a boy alternately. The suggestions for children creating their own ground rules for group discussion is well documented on the QCA/DfES (2003) *Speaking, Listening, Learning* video, which accompanies the printed materials.

For older children in Key Stage 2, putting hands up is not always necessary for taking turns. By Year 6, the children have become so used to the 'rules' that shouting out is rare and a different sort of discussion follows. This is called 'open forum' and is used in circle time and discussion of the day's 'puzzling question'. It is surprising how well mannered these precious 'talk' times are and the amount of respect for each other's opinions the children develop.

It is during these times that the teacher should try to hold back and assume that children have something important to say – they nearly always have. Remember, too, you should respond to their questions as you would to an equal: 10- and 11-year-olds quickly sense if they are being patronised.

When Jamie asked me the God question, I gave the typical teacher's 'sitting-on-the-fence' answer, and immediately knew by the look on his face that I had let him down. He needed more honesty. I did not help him to make sense of his learning. The question, 'Do you believe in all that God stuff?' came when I was sitting with a group of children who were discussing and writing prayers, and he really wanted to know what I thought. I should have given him an 'I wonder?' answer.

Activity

A child in your class asks you if you believe in God. Consider your response. How would you answer the child? Does it matter what sort of response you give? Would it be better put as an 'I wonder?' question to the whole class?

Comment

When asked this question, it is important to know your children and be sensitive to their own beliefs.

Creating an environment and atmosphere in your classroom that stimulates Speaking and Listening

With the advent of more discursive and interactive teaching strategies in literacy and numeracy, children are hopefully becoming more active listeners and more confident in articulating their learning. However, this does not happen automatically, and the teacher needs to create a wide range of 'talk' opportunities and stimuli.

Interactive displays

In common with most primary teachers, I like to have my classroom divided into different areas with lots of interactive displays where children can handle a variety of artefacts. These range from a collection of wooden objects, books and pictures related to science work on materials, to a 'mystery object' relating to a different curriculum area each week. The displays have lots of objects that the children have brought in themselves, and questions relating to them are raised about a specific area of study. I try to change them frequently as the children enjoy fresh displays they can contribute to. The best displays are, of course, created by the children themselves where they have a choice of books, artefacts and visual materials. They will often surprise the teacher with challenging questions and creative ideas for encouraging discussion. However, the children will need to discuss their own criteria for what makes an effective display and the teacher will need to be a good role model for creating an effective learning environment.

While studying the Victorians in Year 5, we borrowed a collection of 'mystery objects' from the local museum and we learned a great deal together. It was surprising how many questions arose from close examination of a carpet beater!

- Is it a fly swatter?
- Was it to hit naughty children?
- Was it for making jam?

'Bags of ideas': Talking Tins, Curiosity Kits, Story Baskets

These are highly motivational and have been successfully promoted and developed in schools in Milton Keynes by imaginative and enthusiastic teachers and teaching assistants in Key Stages 1 and 2, based on an early years concept of 'prop' boxes and Maureen Lewis's research on non-fiction Curiosity Kits (Lewis 2003).

Talking Tins are interesting tins that contain artefacts to stimulate children's interest either in place or character or a mixture of both. The first example was a panecotta tin from Italy, beautifully decorated with scenes of Venice. This was filled with guide books from Italy, museum and gallery tickets, postcards, old Italian Lire and some clues to two characters who have a need to communicate. Other tins have been bags: a mountaineering rucksack with ropes, maps, compass, etc.; a builder's bag with tools, house plans, hard-hat, etc. Some tins have been baskets with photographs, postcards, hats from the First World War and others have been boxes such as an old rosewood box with a rusty key, containing leaflets from Bletchley Park and messages in code; all to encourage talk about the objects, the people, the places and the connections between them.

Curiosity Kits are explained in the excellent booklet published by the Reading Centre for Language and Literacy, and are primarily to stimulate boys' interest in reading non-fiction. They take home a rucksack with a non-fiction book, say about motor bikes, a magazine related to the subject and a model motorbike. They then talk about these at home and, hopefully, share the book and the magazine. One teaching assistant working with a Year 6 boy with emotional and behavioural difficulties found Curiosity Kits the ideal way into supporting a potentially difficult child. She discovered he had an interest in pigeons, and even kept one of his own in his granddad's pigeon loft in Luton. She made up a Curiosity Kit with images of pigeons, a practical guide to caring for pigeons, two stuffed toy white doves and the book *Home in the Sky* by Jeannie Baker. Their relationship was established through talking about the kit.

Story Baskets are an extension of the idea of Story Sacks for younger children and never fail to engage the most challenging youngsters. I was invited to a reading week where visitors were reluctant to visit one particular Year 6 class, due to their challenging behaviour. I took in the story *The Silver Swan* by Michael Morpurgo, in a basket with a large toy swan, a large fox hand puppet, some white swans' feathers, a fishing rod and three toy cygnets. We talked and held the toys before I read the story, some specially 'chosen' boys holding the feathers. All was fine – there were even some tears.

I think this session worked well for several reasons:

- I was a new face.
- The props and choice of text were engaging.
- We created a 'dramatic' atmosphere through talking about the swan and the fox before we read the book.

Useful resources

Building up your collection of resources which encourage and accommodate talking activities is time well spent. Here are a few suggestions that I have used successfully:

- a rug or carpeted area for 'on-the-floor' discussions, story and poetry-reading sessions can help to make the talking area comfortable and inviting; the addition of cushions and bean bags can ring the changes for different 'talk' time; care must also be taken as children spend quite a lot of time in literacy and numeracy, sitting for shared text work, etc.;
- tape recorders, headphones, microphones and good quality tapes for listening to and recording a whole range of work – science and maths investigations, stories and poems, guided museum tours;
- a quiet area to use the above or for role play – this might only be a small screened-off area in a corner of the classroom;

- carefully presented and displayed fiction, poetry and reference books with open questions and suggested activities for the children to interact with;

- recent newspapers for reading and discussing together (replaced regularly) – these could be in the school library or classroom;

- children's own work on display, read aloud and discussed with the whole class;

- telephones, to be used as part of a role-play situation: 'Hello Das, this is Charlie on the mobile. I'll be late for the meeting';

- hats, shawls, etc., for reading and talking 'in role';

- newspaper photographs and art postcards of people talking – my favourite is a postcard of the 'The Whisper' sculpture by André Wallace which is placed outside Milton Keynes Library; it is of two girls deep in conversation – what are they talking about?

- an 'interesting things we've heard' or 'quote of the week' noticeboard – comments collected by children and teachers – overheard or read in newspapers and magazines;

- an ideas box for circle time discussion topics – these can be anonymous and can cover playground or work-related difficulties. Be prepared in the beginning for the occasional 'rude' suggestion – if ignored they quickly stop;

- a range of visual images – paintings, posters, website images, film and video. The British Film Institute (BFI) publishes materials of the highest standard which support a deeper understanding of media literacy but also stimulate talk. Children who may be reluctant to engage with written text may well be motivated by film and visual texts. For further information visit the BFI website at www.bfi.org.uk. They provide some valuable free resources and their website is well worth a visit.

Activity

Choose a favourite story to read aloud, such as *The Wild Washerwomen* by John Yeoman and Quentin Blake (1984), and try using some props to enhance the storytelling – a basket of washing, an apron or the full washerwoman's or woodcutter's costume. Observe the effects on the children and your own storytelling technique.

Comment

Telling a story to a group or class of children is one of the first activities students are asked to try out in the classroom and it can be a daunting task. It is essential to practise at home, reading aloud to the dog, in front of a mirror or into a tape recorder – preferably dressed up!

Teaching and learning strategies

Listed below are several teaching strategies which specifically use speaking and listening as a curriculum focus. They are not exclusive to teaching in the Literacy Hour. Where appropriate

I have made suggestions relating to other curriculum areas. All the suggestions are open to adaptation, variation and development. Many can be found in slightly different forms in related texts and can be recognised as drama, storytelling or poetry-writing conventions. Although these are planned speaking and listening activities, much powerful learning takes place through informal, unplanned, day-to-day talk and discussion. Specifically organised Speaking and Listening sessions should not be the only opportunities for stimulating talk in the classroom. The teacher needs to know her children well before deciding on one particular technique or combination of strategies. Some reluctant talkers become more confident if the teacher sits next to them. This can have the reverse effect on a child who persistently interrupts others. Mixed-ability groups may be daunting for the child with learning difficulties, though sometimes they work very well. Speaking and Listening strategies provide the potential for developing all children's self-confidence and self-esteem. The way children are grouped should be flexible and appropriate to children's needs.

1. Teacher-directed discussion/whole-class teaching

Teaching by careful explaining, questioning and informing are some of the most effective teaching strategies. Interactive teacher-led discussion can involve all the children and can stimulate enquiry and a desire to know more. Shared text work in the Literacy Hour relies on whole-class interactive discussion of text, whether the teacher is modelling writing or during supported composition. Sound subject knowledge is helpful in giving the teacher confidence to answer children's probing and demanding questions. One criticism of the Literacy Hour is that the teacher now does too much of the talking. To ensure a balance is maintained, if you are brave enough, ask a supportive colleague to engage in some peer observation where the focus is on teacher- and child-initiated discussion. The large amount of professional development teachers have received in literacy should raise the quality of talk and understanding in the classroom.

2. Talk partners

This is one of the most successful and easily organised ways of helping children clarify and develop their ideas. It can work with children sitting on the carpet or in groups at tables and can be the preliminary step to working in bigger groups.

Children can simply turn to the person next to them or work with a prearranged partner and talk through their ideas or response to a teacher's question. This is particularly effective as part of whole-class discussion, whether in shared text time or outside the Literacy Hour, and for helping quieter children to feel that their ideas are valued.

Sometimes a time limit can be put on each child's contribution and sometimes the listener can summarise the other person's views to another pair of talk partners. This is an ideal strategy for developing children's listening skills – skills that are every bit as important as the speaking skills. In the heat of the moment children can be so enthusiastic about putting their own ideas forward that they forget to listen to their partner's views.

Working with partners is also an ideal way for children for whom English is an additional language to share ideas in their home language before contributing to a larger group. It can also help their confidence in spoken English if there is no pressure to speak to the whole group.

The role of the teaching assistant both in and outside the Literacy Hour is crucial when working with more reluctant speakers or listeners. She can be a talk partner herself, drawing in reticent children, or she can help keep on task those more easily distracted.

This strategy can be used in all curriculum areas but it is particularly useful in the mental and oral starter in the Numeracy Hour. You can use 'sum talk' as a way of explaining how the children have worked out different calculations. With talk partners children first explain their methods to each other, then – the real test of learning and understanding – they are asked to explain their partner's method to a new partner. In this way understanding grows until everyone understands everyone else. Powerful learning!

3. Developing listening skills

This should be a regular feature of speaking and listening work, even with children at the end of Key Stage 2. Children are encouraged to listen closely to a partner telling them about a particular aspect of learning for three minutes without interruption. They then report what they have heard to another child or group of children. Listening games can also be played in circle time. Children can be encouraged to take notes after watching an educational video rather than during it. You can use a writing framework to help them, along these lines:

- List five things you already know about *The Voyage of Odysseus* before watching the programme.
- Now list five things you have learned about Odysseus's adventures since watching the programme.
- What three things would you now like to find out about Odysseus?

4. Brainstorming

Brainstorming is an effective strategy for initiating discussion, with additional potential as an assessment tool. It enables the teacher to find out more about the children's learning as work progresses. She can assess the children's prior knowledge, what the children are learning and what they have retained about a particular topic. For example, 'What do we know already about the Ancient Greeks?' is an opportunity for children to tell us what they know and that last year they went to Crete and visited Knossos and would you like them to bring some photographs in? It is an opportunity for teachers to assess where the gaps are in the children's knowledge and understanding and which aspects of her teaching have worked well.

Brainstorming does not have to be a group activity. It could begin as an individual written activity and then develop to group or whole-class discussion. Individual thinking time can be really beneficial for some children. Others may need the support of sharing ideas with another child or adult. Different techniques and strategies will work at different times for different children and subject areas.

It is often appropriate for the children to write down ideas they have talked about, either as they go along or after preliminary discussion. Try to provide children with a choice of recording materials. Some like to use large sheets of sugar paper and large felt-tipped pens. Others like to use a whiteboard or an exercise book. However, a favourite method of recording is writing ideas onto an overhead projector transparency, or on an interactive whiteboard, and presenting bullet points to the rest of the class. These can then be added to as work and learning progresses and finally photocopied for everyone as evidence of the children's emerging ideas. A final 'brainstorm' at the end of the Ancient Greek study should provide evidence that real learning has taken place.

5. Review times: Plenaries, 'pit stops' and 'in-flight checks'

These too may be found in classrooms under a variety of pseudonyms. They are integral and crucial to all good teaching and a successful and helpful Speaking and Listening activity. Whichever way a lesson has been introduced – whether by teacher-led discussion, talk partners, brainstorming, practical demonstration or activity – it is important to sustain the dialogue throughout the follow-up work. Sometimes, through lack of time, evaluation of the children's own learning is rushed or becomes a simple sharing of work. This is a missed opportunity for the children's learning to be valued and for them to explain and justify what they have been learning to the class and their teacher. A final plenary session, planned and focused, is an essential part of the daily Literacy and Numeracy Hours, an opportunity to assess whether the learning objective has been met and where the learning needs refining and developing.

A brief 'pit stop' or 'in-flight check' every so often during an activity can ensure that everyone is on task and understands what is expected of them. It can also help those children who find it difficult to get started. Just hearing someone else's opening paragraph or seeing the beginnings of their gymnastic sequence can help motivate and stimulate ideas. Such reviews can help the teacher pick up on misunderstandings and may help her decide who needs extra support during the lesson. If children know there will be a short review time early on in the lesson, this acts as a motivating force to make early progress.

A much later review time, half an hour or so into the lesson, can be a source of much shared information, thoughts and learning. Each group could be asked to contribute three of their main points or individual children could be asked if they would mind sharing their two best questions, paragraphs or musical compositions.

A final brief review time can take place at the very end of a session where one-sentence summaries of learning outcomes can be shared or one-sentence setting tasks for the next lesson can be reviewed.

Plenaries are not just a valuable strategy in literacy and numeracy. A final review time at the end of the day can reinforce how hard the children have worked and send them home feeling really good about themselves; 'I really deserve to go home and have a rest because I helped plan a really good science investigation' (Charlotte), 'I really deserve to go home and have a rest because I enjoyed my book discussion with Mrs Smith' (Paul).

6. Hot seating

This is very popular with children throughout Key Stage 2. Children of all abilities – not just the more confident speakers – take advantage of its benefits. Individual children are invited to sit in the 'hot seat' and assume the role of a particular book character or unknown person in a photograph or piece of descriptive writing. They then have to answer questions, justify their actions or explain events in their book, photograph or article. (See Chapter 7 on developing drama strategies.)

7. Visits, visiting speakers and listeners

The value of educational visits, visiting speakers and visiting listeners has already been referred to earlier in the chapter. They provide children with a focused stimulus to their speaking and listening activities and many have a highly professional approach. One term at a middle school in Milton Keynes yielded the following visits and visitors:

- a residential visit by Year 5 to Shropshire and the Black Country Museum;
- a professional theatre company performing to the whole school;
- the head teacher visiting Year 4 to talk, as part of the children's RE work, about her leadership role;
- a professional artist visiting Year 5 to share her work and discuss the paintings of the Pre-Raphaelite Movement;
- a walk to the parish church by children in Year 4 followed by a talk and question session by the parish priest;
- a Book Week hosted by Year 4 and enjoyed by the whole school where parents and teachers visited as 'guest' readers;
- the County School Librarian visiting to introduce a book collection of new authors to Year 6 with a follow-up discussion six weeks later;
- a visit to Year 6 by award-winning children's writer Michael Morpurgo to talk and answer questions about his writing;
- a visit to the British Museum by Year 6 to study Ancient Greek artefacts, after which follow-up work was to include a written and taped tour guide prepared by pairs of children;
- a teaching assistant visiting the whole school during assembly time to share her expertise in British Sign Language, leading to the establishing of a 'signing' club in school.

8. Reading inside and outside the Literacy Hour

Since the introduction of the Literacy Hour, the systematic teaching of shared and guided reading in both key stages is embedded in the daily Literacy Hour. Both these strategies rely on children interacting with text in a meaningful way through discussion and questioning and have provided a clearer focus to their reading development. However, there should still be opportunities for further reading opportunities outside the Literacy Hour.

Poetry reading, non-fiction book reading, reading challenges, oral storytelling, reading conferences and discussions could be regular features of extra reading time in school. A time where children can put into practice all they have learned about reading in the Literacy Hour. The children are encouraged to share their reading experiences with each other and discuss details about their preferences and analysis of text with their teacher, teaching assistant, or reading helper. They might keep a detailed Reading Journal or Log where everyone involved in the child's reading can communicate with each other. Children at Key Stage 2 enjoy choosing ways in which to present ideas in their journals which are far more sophisticated than a list of book titles, authors and dates when read. There is an excellent example of the high level of discussion following Year 5 children's reading of *The Firework Maker's Daughter* by Phillip Pullman on the NLS Professional Development DVD (QCA/DfES 2003). A Reading Journal helps link shared and guided reading activities with wider reading at home and in school. The most important contributors to the Journals are the children themselves. For further information about the effective use of Reading Journals see the Milton Keynes English e2bn website (www.cgu.e2bn.net).

Reading challenges could take place once a term and the children decide these in discussion with their teacher. Challenges should be adapted and developed according to the age and reading ability of the child. They can be great fun and a real motivation to read in a different way. A selection of challenges may include some of the following:

- Read an easy book backwards from the back page to the front page out loud to a friend.
- Read as many books as you can in a week by the same author.
- Read a book out loud to an older or younger brother or sister every day for a week.
- Read five non-fiction books about something you know nothing about.
- Read a book your mum or dad read when they were your age.
- Bring in three of your favourite books to read to a friend.
- Tell a special story out loud from memory.

Activity

In discussion with a class or group of children you are working with, find five reading challenges the children would like to meet.

Comment

These challenges can be displayed attractively and it is important that the children keep a record of their challenges and whether they have been able to meet them. They are a real opportunity to help parents remain involved in their child's reading in a lively way, at the same time moving the child to greater reading independence.

A favourite challenge is when the children tell their best story out loud. This need not be a well-known story but could be the child's best 'My Lost Pet' story, or 'My Worst Bike Accident' story or, even better, 'My Getting Lost' story. There can be a real competition to share their stories and a special atmosphere can be created sitting in a circle at the end of the day with the lights dimmed and a candle burning in the middle of the circle.

It is surprising what storytelling skills and talents teachers and student teachers have themselves. A group of undergraduate student teachers planned and performed, individually and in groups, a stunning array of stories, in costume with many hand-made props to support their stories. The students performed a traditional Anansi story, sung and told in dialect, a retelling in Welsh of *The Little Red Hen*, a hilarious spoof of *Cinderella*, a witty and clever recounting of *The Vicar of Nibbleswicke* by Roald Dahl and several more atmospheric and moving traditional folk tales and legends. The students surprised themselves and each other with the depth of storytelling talent within their group.

9. Circle time

Circle time is one of the single most effective classroom strategies for developing the Speaking and Listening curriculum in Key Stage 2. It is a simple strategy to develop the children's confidence in speaking in front of a large group about topics that are designed to raise their self-awareness and feelings about a whole range of issues. It is a strategy that has grown in popularity in recent years and is now a regular feature of many primary classrooms. Some concerns have been expressed about teachers using circle time without proper training. Ideally it should be a whole-school initiative with training provided by 'experts' in the field. However, the simple ideas mentioned below can be attempted by any new teacher or any teacher wanting to 'have a go'.

Circle time may be a regular timetabled session in the school curriculum and is often highly valued by the children. It is effective in enhancing the children's behaviour, attitudes to each other, their learning and, above all, their self-esteem. It is an effective strategy for structuring children's talk in 'talking frames' (Goodwin 2001) and for delivering many aspects of the RE syllabus, the Personal, Social and Health Education (PSHE) syllabus and the Speaking and Listening curriculum.

It is easy to organise and can be attempted by teachers at all levels of experience. It is best to begin with getting the children used to talking, reading or sharing in a circle before moving on to a more formal, structured circle time. To begin with, until your own confidence grows, try reading the class reading book, or sharing a picture book sitting in a circle, perhaps taking turns to read short extracts or discuss aspects of the text or make observations about a historical artefact. Sitting in a circle gives everyone equal status and you should find those children who are sometimes reluctant to contribute will feel more confident to do so in this setting.

A more formal circle time session might last about 40 minutes and could begin with a 'warm-up' game or activity such as 'Granny's Basket' where each child passes a basket round and chooses an imaginary object to go in the basket, selecting an item beginning with the next letter in the alphabet. For example:

> I have a basket (*child 1*)
> What have you in your basket? (*rest of class*)
> I have an aardvark in my basket (*child 1*)

> I have a basket (*child 2*)
> What have you in your basket? (*rest of class*)
> I have a balloon in my basket (*child 2*)

and so on round the class and through the alphabet.

In playing this game, you might notice a distinct improvement in the imaginative contents of the basket and the vocabulary used by the children to name the chosen object.

'Fruit Salad' is another favourite game where the children are named after a particular fruit. The teacher calls out a child's 'name' and she has to change places with someone who is also a banana, apple, pear or grape. When the teacher says 'Fruit Salad', everyone changes places. This is a good mixing game and although I must have played it hundreds of times no child has ever realised what is happening in the game – it is purely chance who you end up sitting next to!

You could then move on to choose a 'talking object' from a selection in the middle of the room. It can be the privilege of a child who has a birthday during that week to select the object from a variety of soft toys, a clay head, a peacock's feather, a large shell, an alabaster egg or a wooden whale. Children may then only speak when holding the 'talking object'.

You begin by asking each child, in turn, to speak about something light-hearted, such as:

> The best thing that has happened to me this week is ...
> The thing I most treasure is ...
> What I'm most looking forward to at the weekend is ...
> The kindest thing I've ever done is ...

No child is ever forced to speak. If they do not want to comment they simply 'pass' when the 'talking object' reaches them.

You can then move on to discuss more serious issues which a child may have brought to your notice beforehand or put in the suggestion box. Children really appreciate this opportunity to express their worries or concerns. They are quite often about playground or lunch-time issues, but sometimes work worries emerge and can be shared with the whole group who may have suggestions to help. An 'open forum' may follow when other children can make helpful suggestions to improve the situation. For example:

> I really don't like it when children swear in the playground.
> I am finding it difficult to concentrate on my work table.
> I am really missing my grandad.

There are certain circle time 'Golden Rules' which the children stick to as if it was a code of honour. They never mention another child in the circle by name unless it is to say something good about them. Anything discussed in the circle remains confidential and no child should be interrupted when speaking.

The session might close with another light-hearted activity such as the 'electric squeeze' where everyone in the circle holds hands and passes round a gentle squeeze.

I have been influenced in my circle time work by the pioneering work of Jenny Mosley, author of several excellent books (see the 'Further reading' section at the end of the chapter) which explain the philosophy behind circle time and make many more excellent suggestions for circle time activities.

The above list gives just a sample of activities planned to enhance speaking and listening across the whole curriculum.

Conclusion

Hopefully this chapter will have provided a few well-tried and successful strategies to stimulate quality talk and effective listening in the classroom. These should be seen as a starting point for the student teacher to develop her own strategies for powerful learning at Key Stage 2. Spending time listening to and talking to children will help you towards an understanding of the power of speaking and listening as a tool for learning.

Further reading

Department for Education and Employment (DfEE)/Qualifications and Curriculum Authority (QCA) (1999) *The National Curriculum: Handbook for Primary Teachers in England and Wales*. London: DfEE/QCA.

Goodwin, P. (ed.) (2001) *The Articulate Classroom*. London: David Fulton Publishers.

Lewis, M. (2003) *Curiosity Kits*. Reading: Centre for Language and Literacy.

Mosley, J. (1993) *Turn Your School Round*. Cambridge: Learning Development Aids (LDA).

Mosley, J. (1996) *Quality Circle Time*. Cambridge: Learning Development Aids (LDA).

Mosley, J. (2000) *More Quality Circle Time*. Cambridge: Learning Development Aids (LDA).

Qualifications and Curriculum Authority (QCA)/Department for Education and Skills (DfES) (2003) *Speaking, Listening, Learning: working with children in Key Stages 1 and 2*. London: HMSO.

Speaking, Listening and Thinking with Computers

Lyn Dawes

Introduction

Computers are designed for individual use, but children in primary classrooms often work at the computer in a group. This is sometimes because of a scarcity of computers in schools, and sometimes because teachers believe that children working in a group can support one another by talking about their work. Teachers may have to supervise several groups simultaneously, so such computer groups are most effective when the members can support one another. But what is it that we really want them to help one another with? Children have to learn to cope independently with problems to do with hardware, software, and ideas. For the teacher, it's the third of these areas which is extremely interesting. Ensuring that children have the opportunity to think about and discuss their ideas with others gives the whole group a real chance to reflect and learn. For this reason, it is important that the talk that goes on between children at computers is primarily to do with thoughts, ideas, opinions, understandings and reasons. This chapter looks at how teachers can encourage such educationally effective learning dialogues during ICT-based activities.

Listening to children talking

Researchers based at the Open University have worked with teachers over the last decade to observe children talking together at the computer. The aim was to listen to children at work using a variety of software in order to identify examples of effective speaking and listening. This chapter draws on the data collected by the research projects (for more information see www.thinkingtogether.org.uk). Transcripts of the recorded talk can reveal how children set about tackling ICT-based activities. For example, below are three transcripts of groups of children talking together at the computer. There are some obvious dissimilarities: for example, the children are not using the same software and Transcript 2 records the talk of two girls, rather than a mixed group. But each of the groups was given the same direction by their teacher – to work together on the task. As you read through each of the extracts, consider the following questions:

(a) Do any of the transcripts contain the sort of talk you, as a teacher, would expect to be taking place while children are working in school?

(b) Are the children functioning as a group? That is, are they collaborating with one another, or do they seem to be working individually?

(c) Are the children considering one another's ideas carefully?

(d) Do the children request information from one another?

(e) Does anyone give a reason for what they say?

(f) Which transcript contains talk of a kind that you think is educationally most valuable? Can you say why?

Transcript 1: Taking turns

Three children – Jade, Lucy and Micky – have been asked to work together to complete some non-verbal reasoning tests which were presented to them as 'puzzles'. They have to choose which one of eight tiles will match a given background pattern.

Micky:	See, I told you!
Lucy:	Shut up, Micky!
Micky:	People will think –
Lucy:	Stop showing off!
Jade:	I know what these are.
Micky:	One, two, three. Now it's my turn.
Lucy:	No, it's not your turn! It was your turn just a minute ago!
Jade:	It's number eight.
Lucy:	Now it's your turn, Jade.
Jade:	Number eight and number seven.
Micky:	Now it's my turn. Don't tell me.
Jade:	That one, Micky.
Micky:	Big, middle, and small.
Lucy:	It's your turn – no, it's my turn. It's that one.
Micky:	That one.
Lucy:	No, that one's already been on.
Micky:	Where, where, where, where!
Lucy:	Stop it! Shut up, Micky!
Jade:	There's loads that haven't been on. There's loads that haven't been on!
Lucy:	Micky, it isn't your turn.
Jade:	It's my turn, actually.

Transcript 2: Does that look better?

Two children, Angela and Bridget, have been asked to work together to compile a page for the class newspaper. They have done some research in the library, and are now sorting out the format of the information on the screen.

Bridget:	Does that look better?
Angela:	OK.
Bridget:	Down, yes.
Angela:	OK, OK.
Bridget:	Does that look all right or too small?
Angela:	OK. What happened to my… it's supposed to be on the first page/second page as well.
Angela:	How does that sound? (*reads quote*)
Bridget:	Yes that sounds good, we have to do something, because we've done animal testing on this, we've got to do something a bit… it's a bit heavy.
Angela:	Yes I know. I'm not going to put it on page three.
Bridget:	Four.
Angela:	I said I'm not going to put it on page three.
Bridget:	Yes I know.
Angela:	… we'll have to scatter a few jokes on this page.
Bridget:	Yes and some of the names quiz.

Transcript 3: Ain't worth it, is it?

Three children – Gavin, Sara and Tammy – have been asked to work together to agree on a suitable outcome for a story which has a moral dimension. The story is about Kate, whose friend Robert has told her that he stole a box of chocolates from a shop, to give to his mother who is ill. Kate has promised not to tell anyone.

Gavin:	(*reads*) Kate was worried. Should she tell her parents or not. Here are some of her thoughts. Stealing is wrong. I promised not to tell anyone. Robert is my friend, if I tell he will get into trouble. Robert is kind. He stole the chocolates for his sick mother. Talk together and decide what Kate should do. Then click on one of these buttons. Does not tell her parents or tells her parents. (*reading ends*) Right we've got to talk about it. (*Tammy looks at Sara*)
Tammy:	What do you think?
Sara:	What do you think?
Gavin:	I think even though he is her friend then, um, she shouldn't tell of him because, em, well she should tell of him, em, because was, was, if he's stealing it it's not worth having a friend that steals is it?
Tammy:	No.
Sara:	Why? I don't agree.
Tammy:	We said why. I think that one as well do you? (*Tammy points to the screen and looks at Sara*)
Gavin:	I think she should tell her parents. Do you?
Tammy:	I think I'm – I think even though he is her friend, because he's stealing she should still tell her parents, and her parents might give her the money and she, she might be able to go to the shop and give them the money.

Sara:	I think um –
Gavin:	– but then she's paying for the thing he stole, so I think he should get the money anyway. He should have his –
Sara:	I think that he should go and tell his mother.
Gavin:	– own money Mum.
Tammy:	– even though she has promised.
Sara:	Because he's, well you shouldn't break a promise really should you?
Gavin:	What's it worth having a friend if he's going to steal?
Tammy:	If he steals. If you know he's stolen if she don't tell her parents then he will be getting away with it.
Gavin:	It's not worth having a friend that steals is it? *(Three-second pause)*
Sara:	OK then.
Tammy:	Ain't worth it is it?
Sara:	Tells her parents. *(Sarah clicks mouse)*
Gavin:	Yeah go on.
Tammy:	*(reads)* Robert stole a box of
Gavin:	A box of chocolates from Mrs Cook's shop.

Comment

The way the children have interpreted the teacher's instruction to *work together* differs widely among the groups.

Transcript 1: Taking turns

In this group, the children are in competition with one another. Little information is shared, and much of the talk is to do with the impossible task of making the turn-taking 'fair'. Each is trying to sort things out in their own way, but their styles of doing so conflict, and the children blame one another for this.

Transcript 2: Does that look better?

In this short extract from a much longer tape containing largely the same sort of talk, the children are working together agreeably. They accept one another's ideas without querying them. It is the sort of talk that goes on between friends who have decided to help one another. The page is being compiled steadily by the girls, with no critical appraisal of its quality or design.

Transcript 3: Ain't worth it, is it?

In this group, the children engage with one another in a serious discussion. They question one another's ideas, and ask one another for reasons to justify assertions they make. This is done in a spirit of open enquiry, and all voices are heard. Opinions are respected. Eventually they are able to reach a decision to which they have all contributed.

Types of talk at the computer

Evidently, very different kinds of talk were taking place between children working together at computers. Three particularly distinctive categories could be identified.

1. Disputational talk

This is characterised by disagreement and individualised turn-taking. There are few attempts to share knowledge or to offer suggestions. There are short exchanges which consist of assertions and challenges or counter-assertions. The participants are in competition with one another, and each seems to have strong, but unstated, ideas about what constitutes winning. Transcript 1 is a clear example of disputational talk.

2. Cumulative talk

The speakers build positively but uncritically on what the other has said. This sort of talk is characterised by repetitions, confirmations and elaborations, as in Transcript 2.

3. Exploratory talk

The group engages critically but constructively with each other's ideas, and statements or suggestions are offered for joint consideration. These may be challenged, but justifications are expected and given consideration. Alternatives are offered and reasons requested, with knowledge being shared, and reasoning more evident in the talk. Progress emerges from the eventual joint agreements that are reached, and any decisions 'belong' to the entire group, as in Transcript 3.

Further discussion about these varieties of talk may be found in Mercer (1995). Not all talk fits neatly into this categorisation, but this offers a practical way of distinguishing the sort of talk that teachers say they wish to hear in their classrooms.

Teachers often specify 'exploratory talk' as the sort of talk that they would particularly want to encourage between children working in groups, at the computer or during any other task. However, disappointingly little exploratory talk may take place unless children know that this is an aim for their work together. Computer tasks are motivating and the children may work steadily, but their talk may be largely to do with managing the issues of turn-taking, with unquestioning agreement or disagreement, or with reaffirming their own social position in the class. Children may not be aware that the best use of speaking and listening is as a tool for exploring one another's ideas, or to reason together.

The value of exploratory talk

What is it about exploratory talk that makes it such an important sort of interaction? And if a teacher hopes or aims to encourage exploratory talk between children in her class, how can she help them to achieve this?

First, let us look at the other two types of talk described above. Cumulative talk is appropriate in many circumstances in classrooms, where uncritical agreement is all that is required to complete a task. Children completing a puzzle, or collaborating to present a joint piece of work, would do well if they talked this way. Its strength is that it draws on the friendship and mutual trust of its participants, who are 'easily pleased' with one another, and agree to each other's ideas without examining either the idea or their own response to it. However, the very *strength* of cumulative talk is its weakness when it comes to the crucial stages of problem solving or decision making where agreement is reached without reasons being properly considered. There is no evidence of rational thinking in cumulative talk. That is not to say that the children are acting irrationally, but that they are not making their reasons explicit to one another. If asked, they might well be able to articulate their reasons for assertions and suggestions, but in cumulative talk they make no attempt to do so, and are not encouraged to do so by their workmates. The talk, and the engagement with the task, is superficial.

Interthinking

It is useful to reflect on the effect that working with a partner can have on the child as an individual by considering your own experience of talk about work. Talking with a partner is an opportunity to put half-formed ideas into words. Having to say what you mean – thinking aloud – is a way of making your thoughts clear to yourself; and having to explain and describe things to a partner is a way of developing a shared understanding of ideas. If your partner is prepared to accept your initial suggestion, without you having to justify or defend it, you have no stimulus to engage critically with your own thoughts. Also, you have no alternative suggestions to produce the creative friction from which new ideas arise. This *interthinking* – the joint engagement with one another's ideas to think aloud together, solve problems or make mutual meaning – is an invaluable use of spoken language (Mercer 2000). Children need to learn how to do this, and need lots of opportunities to practise.

Rationality is also not apparent in disputational talk. Children challenge one another's knowledge without offering reasons, and disagree with one another's ideas without offering alternatives. By rejecting ideas they appear to reject the person suggesting the idea. Looking back to Transcript 1, you can see that Micky made many suggestions that were not accepted. If he had been given reasons for the rejection of his ideas, or asked to justify his opinion, then the discussion might have helped him to clarify his thinking. He might have begun to understand why some ideas are more acceptable than others; he might have learned something. And if all three children had considered their own reasoning, their talk together would have had a purpose more crucial to the development of their thinking than that of simply trying to do the puzzles.

Exploratory talk allows a reasoned exchange of ideas and opinions. This sort of talk is likely to be of great value to the children educationally, because it means that they are using language to think rationally, and to consider and evaluate each other's ideas in a cooperative way. They can build up shared knowledge and shared understandings, as they engage in opportunities to collaborate as equals. Collaborative talk of this kind provides a supportive context for thinking aloud, and thinking aloud is crucial if children are to formulate their thoughts and ideas. It also represents the kind of rational, considered debate at the heart of 'educated' activities such as science, law and politics. Engaging in interthinking through rational discussion with other people is likely to help children develop clearer ways of thinking to support their development as an individual.

Encouraging exploratory talk

Exploratory talk is difficult enough for adults to achieve and it cannot be assumed that it will come naturally to children. Some children in primary classrooms may be familiar with exploratory talk from their prior experience in and out of school. They may be capable of using such experience as a model for their talk with their peers. Other children who have relatively little experience or awareness of exploratory talk may be completely unfamiliar with using rational discussion as a means of resolving conflicting views or negotiating a joint solution to a problem. Unlike reading, writing, science and mathematics, talk is learned informally and is in constant use; its very familiarity may make it 'invisible' as a tool for learning. It may not occur to children that the way they talk to other people makes a difference to what they achieve. They may need to be guided into understanding how different ways of talking together can produce different outcomes in their work, and in their life beyond the classroom.

Simply grouping children to work together at a computer will not necessarily help them to develop talking skills. Computers provide rich resources for collaborative work. The sleeve notes with educational software may assert that its use will encourage discussion. But unless children know what we mean by 'discussion', and have the skills to engage one another in speaking and listening, they may gain little of educational value from the talk or the activity. The computer can provide an excellent environment for practising exploratory talk, once this way of talking has been introduced to the children. Apart from offering interesting software, the useful thing about computers is that they are very patient! But children used to game play will rush through programs, heedless of chances to reflect and consider. However, a group of children who are aware of the importance of talk have a real advantage. They can look at the screen, sit back and talk and think together about what decision to take or what to do next. It is the inclusion of discussion in the interaction between children and computer that has real educational potential (see Wegerif and Dawes 2004 for more on this IDRF (Initiation, **Discussion**, Response, Feedback) effect).

When grouped at a computer, it was evident that some children can talk confidently, but not listen carefully to others. Others shy away from engaging one another in protracted talk, as if they find any difference of opinion very worrying, and are unable to distinguish a sensible discussion from a more threatening argument. Still others use ways of being generally agreeable, or disagreeable, to remain uninvolved, while some simply dictate or ask for orders. Some or all of the following problems may arise when groups work at the computer:

1. The children may understand what is required by the program, but they do not understand the intended purpose of their talk together. They do not know how to negotiate with one another, and using the computer will not teach them this directly.

2. Self-appointed group leaders emerge and impose an inappropriate style of working on the group. Those with home computers are proficient with the keyboard and used to playing games where speed is more valuable than talk or cooperation. Keen to show their skill, they dominate the group.

3. Friends tend to agree with one another on principle, and less confident children make no contribution at all, to avoid being held responsible later on. Difficulties with the program and each other may cause some children to withdraw from the group.

4. Encouraged by the game-play feel of some software, talk may be of a casual or social nature. The children may engage in their constant testing and re-establishment of the class 'pecking order'; this process dominates the talk.

It is the role of the teacher to be aware of these effects and to overcome them on the children's behalf. Computers currently retain their popularity and motivating power in classrooms, despite their tendency to unreliability and their capacity to lose hours of work in moments. Teachers have poured much effort into generating good practice with ICT across the primary curriculum, so that computers really can support the achievement of learning objectives. It remains the case that the educational value of work at the computer is profoundly dependent on context, and that it is the teacher's framing and organising of computer-based activity that makes the most difference to achieving learning outcomes with ICT.

Teaching ground rules for talk

A crucial part of the context requiring teacher input is that children who are expected to work together in a computer group need to be taught how to talk to one another. They need direct instruction in the talk skills which will enable them to get the best out of their own thinking and that of all the other members of their group. They need to understand and share the aims for their talk. They can use the computer to practise discussion skills only once they have been taught what the elements of those skills are. They must understand that if all the group can agree on a set of rules, 'Ground Rules for Talk', then talk can proceed in a way which will make the whole group, and its individuals, more likely to achieve success and develop new ways of thinking.

Ground rules which can enable a group to discuss things with one another may not be entirely obvious to children. They have to be disentangled from other rules for talk that they will have learned, or at least heard of. Asked for their ideas about rules for talk, children may suggest:

> Only speak when you are spoken to.
> Be quiet in the library.
> Don't interrupt an adult.
> Don't use bad language.
> Don't shout in the classroom.

Useful as these may be, they are not relevant to engaging in interthinking. Ground rules for discussion are to do with active listening, thoughtful speaking and respectful collaboration. The next part of this chapter suggests a way of teaching talk skills.

Talk Lessons

These are the ground rules for exploratory talk:

- everyone in the group is encouraged to contribute
- contributions are treated with respect
- reasons are asked for
- everyone is prepared to accept challenges
- alternatives are discussed before a decision is taken
- all relevant information is shared
- the group seeks to reach agreement.

The 'Thinking Together' approach (Dawes *et al.* 2000) takes this set of ground rules as the basis for learning objectives for a set of 'Talk Lessons'. One special aspect of these lessons is that at the start of each lesson, the learning objectives for speaking and listening are made explicit to the children. Children are grouped in threes, usually mixed ability and gender. The Talk Lessons initially raise awareness of the importance of classroom talk. Subsequently the groups undertake activities designed to encourage group cohesion and trust. Next comes a crucial lesson in which the entire class discusses and agrees a set of class ground rules for talk. After this, there are opportunities to put the new ground rules into practice, and to undertake further work on each separate skill such as questioning, sharing information, active listening, giving reasons and negotiating group agreement. For example, you can see that for learners there is a progression from not giving reasons, to giving reasons, to giving and evaluating reasons, to agreeing on what is a good reason and understanding a range of points of view, to accepting the reasons of others. Each step on the way merits a separate lesson to establish the idea and to try it out in practice. The invaluable contribution of ICT in this process is to provide motivating and exciting contexts for discussion. (The Thinking Together lessons for Key Stage 2 can be found in Dawes *et al.* (2000); Key Stage 1 lessons are described in Dawes and Sams (2004). For more information see *www.thinkingtogether.org.uk*.)

The first set of Talk Lessons was taught in 1989. The lessons have been in use in classrooms across the UK ever since. Teaching Thinking Together supports the objectives of the QCA/DfES (2003) *Speaking, Listening, Learning* initiative. Thinking Together has been shown to help raise achievement in Key Stage 2 Standard Assessment Tasks (SATs) and in specific curriculum areas such as mathematics and science. This seems to be because, by learning to talk with one another, children learn to think and reason in a way that feeds into their general capacity to do better in the classroom. This is very pleasing; but the lessons were originally used because children's inability to articulate their ideas to one another seemed to make them unhappy in class, and so unable to benefit from learning together. The loss of self-esteem caused by disputational talk and the loss of motivation caused by cumulative talk mean that computer-based activities are superficial – a great waste of the potential of both children and technology.

To work more effectively as a group, children need to be taught how to talk to one another in a way that is both impersonal and intimate. It is impersonal because once children have mastered the structures of exploratory talk they can use it with anyone; intimate because such talk establishes mutual trust for the sharing of ideas, giving children direct access to one another's thoughts.

Below are the ground rules for talk created and agreed by a Year 5 class. You might like to compare this child-speak version with the rules given earlier in this chapter.

Our rules for exploratory talk:

1. We will talk together to think about what to do.
2. We will share what we know with each other.
3. We will ask everyone to say what they think.
4. Everyone will listen carefully to others and consider what we hear.
5. We will give reasons for what we say.
6. We will pay attention and try to think of good ideas.
7. We will decide what to do only when everyone has said all they want.

The effect of the Talk Lessons

Classes using ground rules for talk show a marked improvement in the quality of the children's talk at the computer. In the research project this was confirmed by analysis of videotapes of the children working. After the Talk Lessons, more examples of exploratory talk were evident in the video recordings. More time was spent on talk before decisions were made. Reasoning was evident in the talk; children were using phrases such as, 'I think...' 'because...' 'yes, but if...' and 'what do you think?...' more frequently.

In any mixed-ability class, some of the children will develop their discussion skills quickly during the direct teaching programme, while others will find it hard to listen, hard to talk, or hard to think of reasons for their assertions. Such children may need a little longer and a little more practice; the growing skills of their classmates can act as a model and a reminder. The video evidence shows that many talk-trained children learn how to negotiate their ideas so that they are able to consult the other members of the group and give proper attention to their views. They can ask one another for opinions, and make their own reasoning explicit in their talk. Members of a group have a joint understanding of the importance of their talk and learn to support one another's attempts to discuss ideas and reach a joint conclusion. The Year 5 children discussing Kate's Promise, 'Ain't worth it, is it?' (Transcript 3), were recorded after a ten-week course of Talk Lessons.

Children work together at the computer more effectively once they have learned how to talk to one another in this way. Computers provide an extremely useful and motivating means of practising exploratory talk, once it has been initiated by a programme of Talk Lessons. Many children are adept at discussion and reasoning but others are not, and children who are isolated in their ability to reason may quickly resort to a less taxing disputational style, even though it is obviously more frustrating. Once a class, or most of a class, has exploratory talk in its repertoire, the individuals can work with each other, because the 'rules' are clear and have been agreed in advance.

The Talk Lessons had another interesting outcome. The children who had undertaken the programme also showed an increased ability to solve reasoning problems both working in a group, but also on their own. The research team associated this effect with their better use of critical questioning. That is, children seemed to have 'internalised' the kind of reasoning that they had been doing in their groups. Because they had been required to reason aloud, they could now use this skill individually to reason when faced with an individual decision.

Some computer programs, such as spelling games, tables practice or word processing, do not require group collaboration through talk. But it is useful to teach the Talk Lessons anyway, because the rationality required by exploratory talk is a vital tool that the child can use in all areas of the curriculum. In addition the Talk Lessons fulfilled my aim of helping children to get on better with one another. The class had found their collective voice. They could employ the powerful tools of spoken language to interthink – and so enjoyed their work better and became much better at understanding one another's points of view. Self-esteem and a calm mind are essential requirements for steady development and learning. Thinking Together helped the class to contribute to one another's progress through enjoyment of learning and of one another's company.

Developing awareness of the quality of talk

This chapter has described how some of the talk that goes on around computers can be understood, and has suggested one sort of intervention that has been found to produce a measurable change in the quality of children's talk. This section offers further examples of talk around the computer for you to consider, with brief notes about their context, and comments for you to compare with your own ideas.

Some children may encourage one another to think of the time they spend at the computer as some sort of play time. They may amuse themselves by typing 'naughty' words or by thinking of ways to make the work more like a game. Their talk is as it would be when using a computer at home, and is to do with amusing each other and reconfirming friendship and shared values. Of course this sort of talk is essential in its usual setting, but bringing it into the classroom is an effect that computers can create. Because the computer 'allows' it children may, for example, include cartoon-type violence in stories. In the following extract, Adil and Morgan are using a program in which they can select objects and people from a bank of pictures, and write a story for their choice of illustration. Before this conversation occurs, they have already created a girl character who crashes her boat into some rocks and drowns. The 'dead body' remains on the screen for some time. Their (boy) character moves into a cave as Adil and Morgan continue writing together.

As you read through the talk, consider these points:

- Are the boys 'on task'?
- Does this talk fall into any of the categories described as cumulative, disputational, or exploratory (remembering of course that there is much talk that cannot be categorised in this way)?
- Do you think the boys are enjoying writing their story?
- If you think they are, can you think why?
- If you think they are not, can you think why?

Transcript 4: Skeleton

Adil:	You get to a cave and wander in
Morgan:	Yeah (*reads*) As you are not the cleverest person in the world (*laughs*)
Adil:	(*still typing*) You get lost. You ask the goblin (*points to screen*) for help ... yeah?
Morgan:	Yeah. But then his friend jumps on you and kills you ... and that could be the end of you
Adil:	Yeah
Morgan:	And then we have to go the other way – yes – no – and you chop his head off or something
Adil:	You ask the (*typing in*) goblin for help ... and while your back is turned the skeleton jumps on top of you and kills you
Morgan:	The skeleton jumps on top of you but you knock him off
Adil:	Yes
Morgan:	You knock him off
Adil:	His body is scattered over a large area
Morgan:	But he pulls himself together and goes to sleep on the rock
Adil:	(*typing*) He sneaks up behind you
Morgan:	And you –
Adil:	I think it would have been best if we had seen what the proper one was (*reads*) the skeleton sneaks up behind you (*typing*) It leaps on top of you ... but you manage (*types* 'to knock it off and')
Morgan:	Has that page got enough? Knocks it off ... oh
Adil:	(*typing*) Bones fly evrywhere (*sic*)
Morgan:	Fly everywhere. Is that how you spell 'every'?
Adil:	All right ... all right (*corrects spelling by inserting a second 'e'*)
Morgan:	I was just wondering. It looked a bit weird
Adil:	Knock it off and bones fly everywhere
Morgan:	And then it picks itself up and pulls itself together

Comment

The children are completely engaged in their writing task. Much of the talk is cumulative. This sort of collaborative talk enables both of them to contribute to a joint outcome; they can rely on their partner to agree with their ideas, with little reflection. They are enjoying making up what is a sort of mild horror story with content that is slightly subversive! This collusion is more likely to occur between friends, and while it is perfectly possible for boys and girls to be friends, most children choose a 'best friend' who is the same sex as themselves. Pairs of friends of either sex will tend to engage in cumulative talk. This is pleasant for them and can result in good finished work for some sorts of tasks. But if the task set by the teacher requires problem solving, friends working together might not be the most productive grouping. And if the aim for the talk is that the children elicit reasons and counter-reasons, the same is true.

In the following extract, Hannah and Lisa, both aged nine, are using the art package 'Paintspa'. They are drawing a house in a field by a river, to go with a story that the class has been putting together.

As you read through the transcript, consider the following questions:

- What do you think each child is aiming to achieve?

- Do their aims coincide?

- Do you feel that these two girls are friends, in the way that Angela and Bridget are in Transcript 2?

- Are the children 'on task'?

- Do you think they will leave the computer feeling content with their work together, and satisfied that it reflects the effort they have put into it?

Transcript 5: Rubbing out

Hannah:	I love doing rubbing it out. Do you?
Lisa:	Hang on
Lisa:	Oh yeah. I don't need to. I just need to take a square
Hannah:	a square
Lisa:	Why have we come down? (*inaudible*) Hannah it's not working. Now. Where are you?
Hannah:	Better (*inaudible*)
Lisa:	Hey I've found it and you pushed it away. Plonker. Eh, eh, oops. (*inaudible*) When we ... that's better, ain't it? Let's go along a bit more yeah? Along a bit more
Hannah:	No, no, no that's it. It's that
Lisa:	(*inaudible*)
Hannah:	Across now. Across. Stop. Across. Stop. Down
Lisa:	(It says) undo. It doesn't matter about that bit. So we just need to go down
Hannah:	Go down. Let me do this bit

Lisa:	No, I want to do it
Hannah:	Ah, ah. Down. Across. Right now let me do this one
Lisa:	Oh what. We want to do the river, don't we? We want to do the river now
Hannah:	Not yet. Not yet
Lisa:	I want to do the river. I want to do the river first
Hannah:	You can't. We ain't done the boat
Lisa:	I'm doing the river
Hannah:	Not on there. The river's going to be that...polluted river
Lisa:	I know. I've got to go all the way back to that thing just there and then we've got to go up, haven't we?
Hannah:	Yeah. No we've got to go down and across a bit
Lisa:	Um
Hannah:	Across. Across more
Lisa:	Ohh
Hannah:	There not much more across. Oh come on
Lisa:	We've got to have one of these each, ain't we
Hannah:	You want to do it now? (*singing*) Would you like to swing on a star bum bum bum carry moon beams swing on a star um um um. Would you like to swing on a star ow ow ow
Lisa:	I like these (colours)

Comment

Hannah and Lisa have been asked to work together on a picture. But they cannot agree on anything that appears (or disappears) because they have not shared their conception of the finished product with one another, and are not doing so as they go along. It is interesting how disputational talk like this can be part of a creative process, in that a finished product results; but the creation entails what appears to be a high level of frustration. It appears that neither of the children will feel ownership or pride in the finished result, since it is not what either of them wants separately, and they are not collaborating in a way that would make it a satisfying joint enterprise. They do not negotiate ideas or ask one another for reasons. The role of the computer in this scenario is overtly to provide the means of constructing a picture, and covertly to be a third party, reflecting the wishes of whoever had hold of the mouse last.

The children will no doubt have work to show but they will not have extended their talk repertoire or practised special and useful talk skills. This is fine, as long as the teacher is aware that it is the case. If the children are fiddling around at break time, trying to see how the program works, this sort of disputational talk might be acceptable. But in the context of a school day, in which a 'turn' on the computer is still something of a privilege, it is perhaps a waste of the children's time. And they certainly display signs of being slightly disengaged by the end of this session. But they have not given up. This persistent effort in the face of continual failure to master the program, and constant unhelpfulness from their partner, is a tribute to the motivating power of the computer, and of course to the determination of the individuals. If their individual commitment had been directed into a group effort, and their talk disciplined towards negotiation, they might have succeeded better.

Activity

Record a group of children working together at the computer. Listen to the tape. Can you pick out examples of the three types of talk mentioned in this chapter? How much exploratory talk happens? Which of the children is most adept at facilitating this sort of talk? How can the incidence of exploratory talk be increased?

Most children do their best to collaborate with their partner most of the time, but they may not know how to negotiate with another child whose agenda for the shared activity is very different from their own. The social positions held by boys and girls are naturally extremely important to them, and their interactions inevitably contain an element of awareness of this. Effective talk can help individual children to truly collaborate, that is to express their own ideas lucidly and at the same time find out what their workmates are really thinking about the task in hand. The advantage of teaching about talk, that is teaching children how to question one another, negotiate ideas, share information, and attempt to reach a reasoned agreement, is that the ground rules underlying the ensuing discussion help to avoid the effects of gender conditioning, friendship groups, and other social brick walls that prevent children learning. It's important to be aware of the different ways that children may approach group work at the computer, and the problems that may arise because of the behaviour they bring to the task. Encouraging children to become aware of their own perceptions of one another may help as a strategy for discouraging prejudice which possibly has its origins in simple thoughtlessness.

Exploratory talk in action

In Transcript 6 we join Alana, Reece and Malik who are working with Granada Science Explorer to investigate materials. Their task is to predict and test which type of paper can best be used to block out light. These Year 5 children are members of a class who have worked through the Thinking Together Talk Lessons. The class had created a set of ground rules for talk.

As you read this extract, consider the following questions:

- Does the transcript contain the sort of talk that you would like to happen in your classroom?

- Can you identify any of the features of exploratory talk, or see where the children might be drawing on their ground rules for talk?

- Do you think that this dialogue would help each member of the group to further their understanding of the science concept areas of fair testing and transparency of materials?

- How well is the software supporting the group talk?

Transcript 6: Switch it on and talk together

Alana:	Switch it on and talk together
Computer:	Which do you think will keep out the light most? What do you think? Say your reasons why before you click on a button
Reece:	What do you think then? Writing paper –
Malik:	Black, black (*pointing to screen*)
Reece:	– wallpaper, black paper
Alana:	I think black paper because it's dark –
Malik:	Yeah –
Alana:	– and light can't go through it because it's dark and it's solid
Reece:	What about wallpaper?
Malik:	No
Alana:	(*to Reece*) What do you think?
Malik:	I think black paper
Reece:	I'll go with black paper
Malik:	Yeah, I agree
Alana:	Why do you think that?
Reece:	Because it's black –
Malik:	Because it's black and it's dark
Reece:	That's what I was just going to say – um –
Malik:	And it's really – and you can't see through, light –
Alana:	So – do we agree?
	(*A few minutes later*)
Computer:	Talk together and make a prediction about how many sheets of this paper you think it would take to block out the light completely? How many did you agree on?
Alana:	I think one because black paper – same as I said before – dark and solid
Reece:	How much? How much paper?
Alana:	I think one
Reece:	No, two, two. I think about five
Alana:	What? To block out the light completely?
Reece:	But that's bright – it goes up to 'Bright'
Malik:	Ten – ten (*holds up his fingers*)
Reece:	Ten – or a five
Malik:	Ten
Alana:	I think one, because it's dark –
Reece:	It's not that dark
Alana:	Dark, it's solid and I don't think anything would get past it
Malik:	No – ten would be much better
Reece:	Sh – stop arguing OK, or we can't continue
Alana:	I just want to say this. It's not about – how solid – what's much better – it's about using your –

Reece and Alana: Brains!

Alana:	To think. So what do you think –
Malik:	Um I say –
Alana:	Least number?
Malik:	One!
Alana:	Do you agree?
Reece:	I agree

Comment

This is a brief extract from a much longer session in which the children in this group discuss their ideas about the transparency of materials, and decide how to test their predictions. The children are engaged with the task and collaborate well with one another. It's possible to identify features of exploratory talk; the children ask for and consider one another's opinions and reasons. Everyone is expected to contribute. Suggestions are treated with respect and the children check that there is group agreement. No talk is wasted on, for example, who will use the mouse or read from the screen; these issues have been dealt with in advance. The children concentrate on using spoken language to understand one another. We can see that where there are differences of opinion, everyone is aware that thinking together can help the group to negotiate a solution. This transcript provides a good example of the sort of emergent exploratory talk that happens when children are learning how to talk this way. The ground rules are used a little like a script; eventually this way of talking will be better assimilated and the children will be more fluent in their ability to conduct a rational discussion. They will have added exploratory talk to their repertoire of speaking and listening skills. The talk in this session helped all members of this mixed ability group to put to use their understanding of fair testing and of the varying transparency of materials. In doing so, the group completed the testing successfully and left the computer satisfied with their work – and with one another. The software, specially designed with talk prompts, supports the group by reminding them of the aims for high quality talk. On-screen prompts are the ideal, but talk prompts can actually be provided almost as effectively with post-it notes stuck around the screen!

Conclusion

If using discussion skills is one of the aims of grouping children to work together at a computer, then, first, the children must be made aware of this. Secondly, they must be explicitly provided with the skills they will need to generate high quality, educationally effective exploratory talk. Providing Talk Lessons is one way to introduce such skills, with the class creating and agreeing to a set of ground rules for talk which will provide a basis for all their discussions. As a teacher you have the crucial role of raising children's awareness of how to use the powerful tools of spoken language to good effect.

Many factors will influence children's learning at the computer, but their talk will be reliably productive if the children have been taught how to discuss things together, and if they are aware that appropriate talk is one of their aims. Children can be helped to understand that the way they talk to one another is one of the most important parts of their work at the computer. They can be taught that spoken language is a tool for interthinking, and that such talk benefits both their group work and their own personal development.

Social influences, such as gender and friendship ties, may adversely affect talk at the computer, but by encouraging exploratory talk you can help children to work in groups less affected by such forces. Children's strong motivation to work with computers means that ICT-based activities offer an unrivalled opportunity to practise a way of talking and thinking that will serve them well in all curriculum areas and life beyond school.

Further reading

Dawes, L. and Sams, C. (2004) *Talk Box: Speaking and Listening Activities for Learning at Key Stage 1*. London: David Fulton Publishers.

Dawes, L., Mercer, N. and Wegerif, R. (2000) *Thinking Together: A programme of activities for developing thinking skills at KS2*. Birmingham: Questions Publishing.

Wegerif, R. and Dawes, L. (2004) *Thinking and Learning with ICT*. London: Routledge.

Developing Children's Oral Skills through Drama

Carol Smith

Prologue

The purpose of this chapter is to highlight the power of drama in the classroom to develop children's speaking and listening from foundation stage to the end of Year 6. When visiting schools and working with a wide range of children and teachers, one of my first questions to a new group of children is what aspect of literacy they like best. Where the teaching is lively, creative and involves the teaching of drama the children will unanimously reply 'drama!' In other less inspiring classrooms the children may struggle and say 'spelling' or 'handwriting' or, sadly on one occasion, 'colouring in'. Children generally love drama but their teachers may be shyer to dive in and try it. Why? Perhaps they are anxious that they may lose control of the children; perhaps they have never experienced drama themselves and lack confidence; perhaps they think it means moving all the furniture; perhaps they just don't know what they are missing.

The best way to explore the range of stimulating possibilities that drama can provide for developing children's oral skills at any age is not by reading about them in a book but by engaging in some high quality practical professional development held either in your own school or college or run by your LEA or local higher education (HE) establishment. Actually taking part in an extended drama, experiencing the conventions, such as 'role play' or 'conscience alley', first hand, led by an experienced professional such as Paul Bunyan, Drama Adviser for the Northamptonshire Advisory Service, Simon Rigley, English and Drama Adviser from Buckinghamshire LEA or Teresa Grainger, a Reader in Education at Canterbury Christ Church University College, will give you the confidence to extend your drama practice in school or will give you the incentive to 'have a go' for the first time. If that is not possible, then the *Speaking, Listening, Learning: working with children in Key Stages 1 and 2* materials (QCA/DfES 2003) give advice on professional development in school, alongside drama objectives from Year 1 to Year 6 which show clear progression, and provide exemplar teaching sequences supported by video extracts of good classroom practice. Some excellent handbooks to further your knowledge of drama conventions are included in the 'Further reading' section at the end of this chapter.

Find out what drama courses are available in your local area; ask your head teacher or course tutor if you can book yourself on one that you like the look of. If that is impossible, read the United Kingdom Literacy Association (UKLA) booklet, *Drama: Reading, Writing and Speaking Our Way Forward*, by Teresa Grainger and Angela Pickard (2004)

Comment

If you are feeling particularly anxious about aspects of drama teaching, try not to worry. You are probably using several drama conventions in your literacy teaching without realising. The best way to move forward is to build on what you are already doing, keep it simple and grow in confidence as you develop a strong relationship with your children.

In this chapter I will:

- explore the reasons why using drama is a good strategy to develop children's oral skills, imagination, empathy and experience;
- suggest practical strategies that work well for using drama in the classroom;
- give starting points and ways forward for the 'new to drama' teacher.

I will not attempt to define and describe *all* the many drama conventions that support speaking and listening; that would be the job of a separate book. They are well explained and presented in the QCA/DfES (2003) *Speaking, Listening, Learning* materials, in particular the leaflet *Drama – making it work in the classroom*.

Why using drama is a good strategy to develop children's oral skills

The most significant reason is that children find drama activities particularly engaging and enjoyable. So do teachers. It can be an exciting adventure for the whole class and adds a creative, lively element to many aspects of the curriculum. Most children create drama for themselves in imaginary play. Some have imaginary friends with whom they role play familiar, day-to-day experiences and new and difficult situations. One five-year-old girl I knew well, Emily, had three very real, to her, imaginary friends – 'Doddy', 'Sarah' and 'Emma' – who had been part of her life since about the age of three. These friends would fill the gaps when other playmates were not around, and would also be a willing, compliant audience for new language and new experiences. Doddy in particular was able to do all the difficult things Emily found hard to cope with. He loved staying on his own at playgroup, he wanted to go to school, he could already swim, skip, and loved having new shoes bought for him. Her parents and grandparents were sometimes invited into the imaginary world with Emily, Doddy and Sarah, but Emily always supplied the script. When grandma was the 'shoe shop lady', Emily told her what to say and grandma had to get the script right. The three imaginary friends disappeared when she went to school because her Reception class was a rich and stimulating place to be with lots of opportunity to share role-play situations with other children and interested adults. If we do not provide these enjoyable situations at school we are depriving the children of an important part of their social and language development. Drama gives children the vital opportunity to explore the language of everyday situations through the role play of real-life situations and also provides the opportunity to experience the thoughts and language of fictional characters. Just how exciting must it feel to assume the role of a fictional character? Real-life role-play situations may well be more familiar in primary classrooms, but by exploring the language of social interaction in the café, vet's or garden centre children can practise the words and accompanying behaviour needed in real life. They can rehearse the language of negotiation, confrontation and organisation in a safe and secure environment.

Another important reason why drama is a powerful strategy for developing children's oral skills and experience is the powerful impact watching live performance can have on children's imaginative and linguistic understanding of their own lives. Whether it is a puppet show, a clown, or a full stage production, the performers are modelling a whole range of voice, dialect, humour and dialogue that impacts the children's imagination and thoughts about their own lives. Being part of a live performance is never a passive activity, unlike watching some television, which makes very little demand on the viewer. Despite this, the impact of good film and television can be an area to explore and enjoy with your class. So much rich talking and writing can follow visits to or visits from live performers. Even being read a good story can be like sharing a mini-performance and can be as appealing and engrossing for the child. It should be every primary teacher's duty and every primary-age child's right, throughout their school career, to read and be read to regularly in an engaging way.

Activity

Book a seat for yourself and a friend at a local theatre for a production that is specifically produced for children. If possible look out for the work of drama in education companies such as 'Shakespeare4Kidz' or 'Cornelius and Jones' and book yourself into one of their workshops. If this is not possible, treat yourself to a trip to the seaside to watch a 'Punch and Judy' show and ask yourself why children still love this traditional puppet show.

Comment

How different did the activity above feel to watching television? What were the children's reactions and responses? What did your friend think? Did talking to him/her about the performance add to your enjoyment? Could you see the value of using live performances with the children you work with? You may be asking questions about the expense of bringing live performers into school and this can be an issue in schools where parental contributions are difficult to ask for. Most performers try to keep their costs to a minimum and it is all a question of priorities.

The final reason why I think drama has an impact on children's learning and developing oral skills is that children are able to construct their own scripted work to entertain and amuse an audience. They can recognise the power of language first hand by having to take into account a real or imagined audience. At one school where I was working, I remember asking a class of so-called 'reluctant and disaffected' Year 6 children if anyone did any writing at home. This was in a school where you would not expect much home interest in reading or writing. Always be prepared to have your preconceptions challenged, as in this particular case. One boy, respected in the class for his football-playing skills, not his literacy skills, Afzaal, said he wrote plays on his computer. His friends and teacher were amazed. It turned out they were comedy sketches – he loved *The Office*, starring Ricky Gervais, and had all the videos and scripts at home. His teacher followed this up, the boy's scripts were read and performed in the Literacy Hour, some friends helped him edit them and he even sent one to the BBC. The BBC took the time to give him some constructive advice, told him to keep writing and that in a few years they would be interested in hearing from him again. This was great motivation for Afzaal, and a great opportunity for the class to explore the language of humour and be responsible for their own production and evaluation of the sketches.

Practical strategies for using drama in the classroom to develop children's oral skills

Many of the ideas suggested below work well; they have been tried and tested successfully in a wide range of classrooms. It must be remembered that drama is not a newly advocated classroom strategy, despite the government's slow reaction to the need to provide some helpful classroom guidance for teachers. I have used the suggestions frequently with a whole range of children at different ages and stages. Some activities work early in the academic year, others work as our relationship with individual children and the class as a whole develops. You will find that some strategies are more successful than others depending on the age and development of the children. Success will also depend on the children's level of drama experience. When working with a range of drama strategies with primary-age children, you need to keep an open mind to the creative outcomes that may emerge.

Props, puppets and performers

I would quickly become bored with my own teaching if I did not have a loft full of props to support many aspects of my work. Many of these are simple and inexpensive, found in junk shops, charity shops, saved from my children's toy collection and stored in boxes and baskets of soft toys, ribbons, old photographs, beanie fish, wooden birds, camouflage netting, beach shelters and puppets.

One team of Years 3 and 4 teachers I was recently working with felt the children's interest in guided group reading had dwindled and they wanted some support with ways to enliven and enrich the experience. The choice of good quality texts is always the first place to look and we did a bit of redistribution and shopping and then put together boxes and baskets of props and artefacts to entice the children into the text. One basket contained four different sets of books about pirates; copies of *The Man Whose Mother was a Pirate* by Margaret Mahy; and six copies of *Captain Abdul's Pirate School* by Colin McNaughton to complement the scheme books about 'Pirate Pete'. In order to read the books, the children had the option to wear eye patches, spotted scarves, a hooked hand, a plastic sword, several parrots on their shoulders and various other stereotypical pirate artefacts. Also in the basket were single copies of non-fiction texts about real pirates such as Ann Bonny, Bluebeard, Mary Read, etc. This idea of 'themed' baskets and boxes was developed throughout the term linked to the text range in the primary Literacy Strategy and hopefully guided reading will never be dull again.

During a recent Year 6 summer school for children from our Excellence Cluster of schools, we planned and prepared a week of English activities linking the Olympic Games held in Athens 2004 with the story of the siege of Troy. From a variety of sources, including extracts from Homer, pictures of Greek pots, some real Greek pots, olive wreaths, posters and trailers from the film *Troy*, various cut up sheets, masks and wooden staffs and books from a Schools' Library Service collection, the children were asked to make a three-minute filmed video presentation of some aspect of their new learning from the week. A fellow consultant and I were amazed at the ingenuity of the children in using the props for their final presentation. We were also interested to see that for both the science element and the Physical Education (PE) element, drama was used as the medium for presentation to the parents at the end of the week.

In Chapter 2 puppets are mentioned as useful props when working with younger children. Children's understanding and learning of phonics can be enhanced through a dramatic presentation. The Early Literacy Support (ELS) video has an excellent example of a teaching assistant working with a group of Year 2 children using a puppet for a Progression in Phonics (PIPs) game. 'Jolly Phonics', too, uses the snake puppet and lively dramatic actions. Both phonic methods use a games and activities approach which is entirely oral – not a phonics worksheet in sight. I have a collection of puppets with moveable mouths. Crow and Dinosaur are particularly effective and the children seem to really believe the puppets are speaking; they are always willing to enter the drama with you. The best supplier of puppets, from child-sized wizards to tiny mermaid finger puppets, is 'Puppets by Post' (*www.puppetsbypost.co.uk*).

Working closely with our Traveller Education Unit, I had the pleasure to be invited to an outdoor performance by 'SNAP', the Travelling Drama in Education group (*www.snaptheatre.org*). They retold, through mime, speech and music, two traditional Gypsy stories that captivated the imagination of all the children in the whole school and acknowledged and paid tribute to the rich Traveller culture. The value of inviting professional performers into school cannot be underestimated. As a result of the visit the children were able to talk to the actors and take part in an afternoon of workshops. The group even provide a support pack of teacher resources for follow-up work. The school gathered a collection of Traveller stories from their own Gypsy children, some recorded in local dialect and to be treasured as a rich oral resource.

Role play

There are many drama conventions that enhance the development of children's oral skills, but I would suggest that one of the most fruitful and accessible to all teachers is role play in all its forms.

Children of all ages and stages love to dress up or be part of a role-play situation, whether to enhance the understanding of a storybook character, or to see a point of view in an argument in literacy or in other curriculum areas. At a familiar level you could start with creating an environment in the classroom linked to a curriculum area, say a shop most children will have visited or will know about. In Year 5, while studying St Lucia, we created a very lively Travel Agents' shop in a corner of the classroom, complete with travel posters and brochures, a telephone and computer. The children booked many imaginary exotic holidays to the Caribbean. They could explore routes on maps, work out the cost of flights and holidays and current exchange rates. All this information came from existing geography resources, supported by data from a daily newspaper and a computer data-handling package. A mother of one of the children worked in a local travel agency and came to talk to us about her job. She was bombarded with questions:

> Do you go to all the places in your brochures?
> What's the most unusual holiday you've booked for anyone?
> How much do you earn?

It was interesting to note that after her visit the children, girls in particular, assumed the additional role of Mrs McGeary in the Travel Shop.

Moving away from the familiar, during work on the Victorians, using screens and artefacts, we set up replicas of Charles Dickens's and Charlotte Bronte's studies. Here, the children wore shawls, cloaks, bonnets and top hats and wrote with quill pens or fountain pens. Surrounded by aspidistras, old copies of the authors' novels and pictures of Queen Victoria, the children were working in a literary and historical environment. The studies became a favourite retreat for quiet work and reading. The children would 'become' the writers, instinctively changing the way they spoke to each other, very politely and formally, wearing hats! Pioneering work has taken place in Liverpool schools on the 'Quiet Place' – a calming and supportive place where children can escape and relax – and I have seen caves, tunnels, bird hides all used as a simple 'quiet place' which provides the right sort of environment for speaking and listening in role if the children wish to. Otherwise it is just a good place to be, a place for children to have 'time out' from their normal classroom routines. In one classroom I visited recently, the 'quiet place' was simply two chairs in a corner with cushions, a tank of tropical fish and magazines and comics; it was a 'waiting room' and children simply assumed the role, language and behaviour of 'waiting', as in a doctor's or dentist's waiting room.

Whole-class or whole-school role-play opportunities can be enjoyed by all and have an imaginative impact on the children's learning and language – it is not easily forgotten and provides a real or imagined context for the language learning. A favourite day in Year 4 is 'Tudor Tuesday'. The children have the opportunity to dress up as pedlars, peasants, archers,

famous Tudor characters and to bring a Tudor lunch wrapped in a napkin. A visiting histor-
ian, Jack Green, who arrives at Milton Keynes station in role, in costume, speaking the
language and dialect of the time, leads the children through a variety of authentic workshops.
All the Year 4 staff and many parents, all dressed in appropriate costume (recycled from
Victorian Day), also lead workshops which include dyeing with natural dyes, dancing a
pavane, and archery.

Much has been written about developing extended role play through working with text
and if you want to plan more I suggest you read *Cracking Drama: Progression in Drama within
English (5–16)* by Paul Bunyan *et al.* (2000) and published by the National Association for the
Teaching of English (NATE). In this excellent book the authors use rhymes such as 'Humpty
Dumpty' for the youngest children in the primary age range working towards more sophisticated texts such as 'The Highwayman' by Alfred Noyes. The book contains well-planned
sequences of sessions with links to NLS drama objectives.

As teachers and student teachers we can all appreciate the value of role play in early years
settings, but role play can cover a whole range of possibilities, from very contained 'small
world' play, where objects, figures, artefacts are brought together in a small container for the
children to play with on a table top, to full-blown whole-school role play. At Rivers First
School in Bletchley, they hold a 'Carnival of Countries' week each year, late in the summer
term, where all the children work towards a grand parade in which they wear costumes and
dance around the school in the style of their chosen country. I was fortunate to be invited to
take part this year and worked with each age group from Foundation to Year 3 on the general
theme of 'carnival'. First of all we read *Nini at the Carnival* by Errol Lloyd and talked about
Bletchley Carnival, which most of the children had seen and some had taken part in. Then we
watched the short animation *El Caminante*, from the BFI materials 'Story Shorts', about a travelling tightrope walker who visits a small town during their fiesta and dramatically entertains
the townspeople with a tightrope-walking extravaganza. Finally we watched a very short
extract from the film *Chocolat*, where the French village is holding a street carnival with fire-
eaters, jugglers, dancers, bunting and balloons and music. I then assumed the role of 'El
Caminante', wearing a long purple cloak, and produced out of my large basket, juggling balls,
tightropes, pretend flames made out of tissue paper covered in watered-down PVA glue and
swirly ribbons for the dancers. To begin with, we practised the skills needed out of role. This
could have taken place in an earlier PE lesson, but I was working within the time constraint of
an afternoon. After we had all had a practice we played and listened to the music *Carnival de
Paris* by Dario G and decided how we were going to organise our carnival. The teachers and
teaching assistants assumed their roles too, and the children took their own roles seriously –
really balancing along the skipping rope, tossing the juggling balls from hand to hand;
pretending to swallow and eat the flames; and spinning and dancing with the swirly ribbons.
One group were the villagers and toured the street entertainers, pointing, laughing and chat-
ting to each other. They had an assortment of hats, shawls and waistcoats to wear and entered
into the role with genuine enthusiasm. In discussion with the staff afterwards we were aware
that the children who were most at ease with being 'in role' were the foundation stage children. The Year 3 teacher said that although her children enjoyed the afternoon they clearly

were less used to working in this way. We then had a meeting to plan more drama activities for the next term, using as support the materials from the *Speaking, Listening, Learning: working with children in Key Stages 1 and 2* (QCA/DfES 2003) document, which has some excellent suggestions for working with story and engaging the interest of an audience.

The concept of whole-school role play can be developed to its fullest extreme in the hands of talented individuals such as Noel McHugh at Glastonbury Thorn First School in Milton Keynes. Here, Noel was the driving force behind the whole school being organised around different termly, themed, role-play environments. As an airport, even the cloakrooms became the luggage handling bases. The classrooms were all terminals and the head teacher's office was air traffic control. The playground was the runway with outside equipment to stimulate imaginary play. The benefit to the children's language development and the improvement of oral skills is immense. However, to make it work, the whole school has to be 'on board' and it is a brave decision to work in this way. The head teacher, Fiona Webb, and all the staff know it works for their children.

Activity

Gather together a few props that would lend themselves to the role play of a particular real or fictional character. Put together an interesting set of artefacts to accompany your favourite book which could be used in a guided reading session.

Comment

Some of the best places to find props, costumes and artefacts are charity shops and car boot sales. Capes can easily be made if you are handy with basic stitching on a sewing machine. If you enjoy going to fancy dress parties yourself you will have no trouble coming up with ideas.

Story, storytelling, Reader's Theatre

Much has been said in previous chapters about the rich source of oral development through storytelling and story. When working with children to develop a more articulate response to their understanding of text, I often use a version of Reader's Theatre. We choose a particular scene where we want to explore further the author's themes, reasons why a character behaves in a certain way or makes a particular decision, or a specific development in the plot. Sometimes we use a freeze frame and comment on what is happening or use some thought tracking; sometimes a group re-enact the story up to a certain point and we do some predicting of what could happen or what the characters could say. On occasions we organise it so that one group directs another, or we have meetings with other characters from other stories who comment in role on what is happening. I don't think I have ever fully explored the full potential of Reader's Theatre. Maybe that is something you will enjoy doing.

Activity

Next time you are reading to a group or class of children, pause at a moment of high tension or high action and ask a group of children to put themselves in a freeze frame of the key scene. Invite the remaining children to try some thought tracking of the characters, ask themselves what each character is thinking at the time. Put one of the key characters in the 'hot seat' and have the rest of the class role play another key character and challenge them in role. Ask the characters some flash back and flash forward questions – what has just happened, happened yesterday, will happen in ten minutes, tomorrow?

Comment

Is this a technique you could use with any age of children? Did it give you a deeper understanding of the text? This is a technique that needs to be used appropriately and sensitively – if overused it ceases to be as effective. The 'hot seating' in role can be really exciting and invariably breaks new ground in understanding of character.

Ways forward

1. Start with what you already do well and build a little drama into it. Start simply and with an element of speaking and listening you already do well. This might be reading stories. Try telling a favourite story instead with a few props. It could be a traditional story you know well or a real-life experience that has happened to you. Alison, an NQT, told a great story during one assembly. It was about getting lost while walking on the Greek island of Simi. She wore the very shorts and T-shirt she had been wearing on the day and children were invited to play the part of her husband, the orthodox priest of the tiny church they had to sleep in over night and the Greek fisherman who finally rescued them. The whole school burst into spontaneous applause at the end and Alison's reputation as a fantastic storyteller grew (Alison had never considered herself a good storyteller until then). What's more it led to a whole spate of 'getting lost' stories being told on the playground, in the classroom and in the staffroom.

2. No matter what age group of children you work with, if you have never done it before, set up a role-play area in your room. Link it either to a story you are reading or a geography or history theme. If you are studying rocks in Year 5, create a Blue John cavern with a beach shelter and some blue and yellow crepe paper, and read the children *Blue John* by Berlie Doherty. The illustrations by Tim Clarey will further inspire you. Hang some thin washing line from the cavern with questions about the text, vocabulary and discussion topics for the team of geologists working in the cavern. Do any of them catch a glimpse of Blue John? Take on the role of lead geologist yourself – wear a hard hat and a head torch and create an atmosphere of discovery in the classroom. It works. I've done it.

    If there is not enough space for an extensive role-play area, try creating a 'quiet place' where two or three children can go and hold a meeting in role between two story characters, say Goldilocks and baby bear or Hogarth and the Iron Man. Alternatively it could be a meeting place for the local residents and the children where the building of a skateboard park is being planned.

3. Begin making a collection of puppets for you to use and a separate collection for the children to use to dramatise stories. If you have time, make stick puppets of favourite book characters. Use a colour photocopier, laminate the picture and attach to a thin green garden stick. Keep a set of stick puppets with a set of guided readers and you have already encouraged children to use the story language in a dramatic context. Easy!

4. Join with a colleague you like and trust, preferably from a different year group, and do some peer coaching. Look at your current planning together and decide on one or two opportunities for using one of the above conventions. If there is supply cover available, try some team teaching, say of conscience or decision alley, where the children make two lines representing alternative views and articulate a reason for or against a course of action. Alternatively enlist the support of an enthusiastic and willing teaching assistant. Give each other feedback and if you are brave enough video yourselves and the children. This is an excellent resource for reflection and review conversations. If you have an LEA literacy consultant working in your school, drama could well be an area he or she would be willing to support you in developing. The consultant may be able to do some demonstration lessons or if you have a team of literacy demonstration teachers in your LEA, there may be a drama expert you could observe. However, nothing is as good as having a go yourself.

Conclusion

This chapter has given some simple starting points for drama in the classroom and primary school. It has shown how these can grow very effectively into engaging tasks which can involve the whole school. Remember the advice at the beginning of the chapter: if you lack the confidence to start, find a drama course or a colleague who can help you take the first important but challenging steps.

Further reading

Bunyan, P. *et al.* (2000) *Cracking Drama: Progression in Drama within English (5–16).* Sheffield: NATE.

Grainger, T. and Cremin, M. (2001) *Resourcing Classroom Drama: 5–8.* Sheffield: NATE.

Featherstone, S. (2001) *The Little Book of Prop Boxes for Role Play.* Lutterworth: Featherstone Education Ltd.

Featherstone, S. (2002) *The Little Book of Treasure Baskets.* Lutterworth: Featherstone Education Ltd.

Featherstone, S. and Featherstone, S. (2001) *The Little Book of Role Play.* Lutterworth: Featherstone Education Ltd.

8

Monitoring and Assessing Speaking and Listening in the Classroom

Lyn Dawes, Lorraine Hubbard and Carol Smith

Introduction

As teachers you have responsibility for monitoring children's progress and keeping records of their development. Talking to our students about assessment we found that many felt less confident about doing this in speaking and listening than they did in other areas. They were aware of the need to incorporate assessment into their planning but often felt that they had few models to follow and that they were not sure what constituted evidence or how to capture and record it appropriately. It is difficult to disentangle the different strands identified in *Speaking, Listening, Learning* (QCA/DfES 2003): Speaking, Listening, Group discussion and interaction, and Drama. It is hard to identify what counts as evidence of development and progression, both for individuals and for your class as a whole. Different aspects of talk can be identified: the social, the communicative, the cultural and the cognitive, all of which are affected by audience, purpose, context and content (Bearne and Elding 1996: 13). Other factors such as gender, personality, interests and confidence in whatever language is used will influence the way speakers behave. Teachers will need to take these interrelated aspects of speaking and listening into consideration in order to develop teaching strategies which incorporate different approaches to assessment.

Planning for assessment of Speaking and Listening

The National Curriculum Programmes of Study and level descriptions for Speaking and Listening are rather generalised. We have to develop a range of strategies for listening to children talking, taking into account a number of features which might not relate to their oral ability. These will include:

- who the child is speaking to
- what sort of task is involved

- previous experience of the talk task
- the child's fluency in a home language as well as English
- the gender of the child and other group members.

We have to note the child's proficiency as a speaker and listener in a very wide range of situations. During a school day they will be required to respond to questions, listen to stories, act on oral instructions, work closely with their classmates and perhaps contribute to class discussion. We need to keep some record of their spoken interactions during the normal classroom day across different curriculum areas. This will involve collecting information on each child from a range of contexts and groupings, over time, and will require a level of observation and recording which can at times seem daunting.

It may be helpful to have a checklist for recording Speaking and Listening activities and to consider some of the following factors:

- what the child knows and understands about the way language works
- the ability to communicate one to one, in or to a small or large group
- the ability to communicate with known and unknown audiences
- the appropriateness of language used in different circumstances
- the ability to interest an audience
- the ability to cooperate, take turns and not to dominate
- confidence, clarity, coherence, audibility
- range, variety and appropriateness of vocabulary
- the ability to reason, argue and debate
- the ability to summarise
- the ability to listen to others in different situations
- the ability to use speech in role play
- the ability to ask questions.

(from Browne 1996: 224)

Accounting for all of these requires meticulous recording. As there is no formal oral test at either Key Stage 1 or Key Stage 2, priority may not be given to the assessment of Speaking and Listening. Reading and Writing may be given much more priority. In addition, because schools have not been required to provide evidence of progression to the same extent as they have for Reading and Writing, teachers may feel less confident about assigning levels and identifying aspects of progression. The SCAA publication and video *Speaking and Listening: Key Stages 1 to 3, Levels 1 to 8. Exemplification of Standards* (SCAA 1996b) addresses this issue. Video extracts show examples of children in different contexts and identify aspects of their speaking and listening which are significant at particular levels. It illustrates the broad lines of progression that are expected: confidence in adapting talk, using standard English when appropriate, listening with understanding, participation in discussion. The video and accompanying document give a general idea of what is required by the Programmes of Study for Speaking and Listening in the National Order for English.

In response to the National Curriculum Orders, we need a focused approach which sees that planning for effective and informative assessment of Speaking and Listening is central to teaching and learning. We must also be aware that making progress in talk isn't just a matter of practising different kinds of purposes for talk. Neither is it having experience of a number of audiences, or even having experience of all the types of talk text listed in curriculum documents. Making progress involves more socially and culturally influenced qualities such as increased flexibility and the capacity to choose how and whether to speak in specific circumstances. It also involves developing the confidence to initiate discussion or support opinion by reference to wider experience.

The primary purpose of teacher assessment is formative, its aim being to improve the quality of teaching and learning as it is taking place; summative judgements which are based on ongoing formative observation and recording will be passed on as feedback to pupils, parents and colleagues at the end of a term or key stage. All the information you record will provide diagnostic evidence that highlights individual strengths or difficulties and this will be the basis for your planning. Assessment should record what children can do and ideally should arise in natural classroom contexts. As far as possible, we should provide assessment procedures that allow children to be active participants in the process and to be able to reflect on their own speaking and listening. Some of the formats that we provide in this chapter are intended for this purpose.

It is clear that, for most children, there is an enormous expansion of learning capacity and language competence from pre-school years to the end of primary education. It is possible to chart some of the kinds of progression, from early to middle years at school, that are particularly evidenced in speaking and listening.

Baseline assessment: providing evidence of children's learning

It is evident that any assessment of pre-school children will have to take place through the medium of speaking and listening. As mentioned earlier in this book, children enter school with considerable experience of speaking and listening. The specification of goals for children's learning in the *Curriculum Guidance for the Foundation Stage* (DfEE/QCA 2000) means that teachers of nursery children will have to plan and assess a range of activities to enable them to produce evidence of individual children's progress towards achieving the Early Learning Goals that will set them on track for Key Stage 1 of the National Curriculum. Much of this evidence will be obtained through dialogue between staff and children, and between children themselves.

> A child's response during a single activity is not always an accurate or reliable guide to underlying competence. Therefore, there needs to be caution about conclusions drawn on the basis of one activity alone. Evidence collected over time from a range of activities is sometimes necessary in establishing what a child knows, understands and can do. Similarly, it is not always possible to infer what a child

can do from observation alone, or recorded work alone. Talking with children has a central role in assessing their understanding, and it is often through talk that a fuller picture of what a child can do is gained.

(SCAA 1997a: 7)

The document *Curriculum Guidance for the Foundation Stage* (DfEE/QCA 2000) is a guide for teachers in nursery units and in the early years of Key Stage 1. It covers areas such as planning, assessment and teaching and sets out what children and practitioners need to do in order to achieve the Early Learning Goals. The nature of the work in the early years means that there is an emphasis on speaking and listening particularly to provide evidence of learning and progression. The 'what' and the 'when' of assessment are not such an issue for teachers but the problem of 'how' remains, given the lack of time and the pressures of daily life in the classroom.

Assessment procedures in two nursery classes

Two nursery schools that we have observed are addressing this issue and recording children's development according to the six areas of learning set out in DfEE/QCA (2000):

- personal and social development;
- language and literacy;
- mathematics;
- knowledge and understanding of the world;
- physical development;
- creative development.

On their arrival in the school, a blank book is provided for each child in which their progress will be recorded. The first page consists of a photograph of the child at home and parents are invited to write down information about their child in response to such questions as, 'What does your child like to do at home?' 'Does your child play with other children?' 'Can you describe your child's personality?' Parents are also asked to write down what they expect their child to gain from the nursery. The book will gradually accumulate a series of photographs taken by the teacher or nursery nurse of the child at work, with written comments by the teacher on what the child is doing. Examples of the child's work, such as drawings, may also be included. A continuous record of the child's progress is being built up, which contributes to summative reports at the end of a year.

The purpose of these books is to record the child's development for the teacher, the parent and the child. The books are of a very personal nature and always available for the child and parent to refer to. Both schools find this an excellent way in which to involve parents in the nursery experience and become aware of their child's progress. There are many significant events during the day that parents do not see, such as playing with blocks, planting in the garden and mixing paints. All these can be photographed and serve as a reminder to teachers and help parents to see and understand what their child is learning in the nursery. One head teacher commented that the value of these books in the nursery was the way in which they could record a range of developments that happen so quickly at this age. Staff and parents can write in the record books; when one child won a swimming award his parent came into school and entered the award in his book. As children are working, staff can observe them, take photographs and note down on a label what the child is doing. Later, the teacher will write by the photograph in the book what the child has been learning in terms of the Desirable Learning Outcomes; targets are set for the child and the evidence of progression is noted. Records are entered in the children's books in the following way:

- observations are made and written in black

- analysis of learning and targets are written in red

- progression is written in green.

Evidence of progression might be that a child becomes able to write their name or when a child speaks in English instead of the community language for the first time. The arrival of a new set of photographs of the children at work provides a talking point, deciding which ones to put in their books and what was happening at the time. Children are able to write in the books and can contribute a drawing; in this way they share in the assessment process.

Both head teachers stressed the importance of this kind of detailed observation in order to record the process of learning rather than focusing on the end product. Although recording this kind of evidence is time consuming – the books are written by staff each week – the benefits are considered valuable by both schools. Parents are particularly enthusiastic about the record books and become highly motivated to contribute to them.

The record books are confidential to staff, parents and children and are freely available for parent or child to read and contribute to. Children love to look at them and often 'read' them during the day. The record books belong to the parent and child and at the end of their time in the nursery the books are taken home and can be shown to the next school.

Frameworks for assessment

Assessment procedures which involve children and their parents or carers in the process can be continued in Key Stage 1 classrooms. One of the most innovative and influential frameworks for the recording and assessment of language development, the Inner London Education Authority's Primary Language Record (Barrs *et al.* 1988), provided a framework for assessment which included input from parents and children. This would seem to be particularly useful in the case of speaking and listening where so much of the child's experience takes place in the home. This record encouraged a two-way communication between home and school, 'to let parent(s) share their knowledge of the child at home and school' (Barrs *et al.* 1988: 12) and required that the child should 'talk about and discuss with the teacher her/his experiences, achievements and interests as a language user' (Barrs *et al.* 1988: 14).

Many of the observations about the problems that are raised when we try to assess development in speaking and listening have not been resolved. 'Keeping a record of children's development in talking and listening may present difficulties not found when recording children's development as readers and writers' (Barrs *et al.* 1988: 20). One of the problems that the Primary Language Record identified was that 'talk disappears into the air'; another was that as teachers we are often part of any classroom interaction both as contributor and as monitor. Added to this is the fact that for many children in our classrooms who are using community languages as well as English, we may not be able to take into account the part played by their first language. More than a decade ago the writers of the record felt that 'adequate ways of mapping children's spoken language development have always proved elusive, mainly because of the complexity of what it is that is being analysed' (Barrs *et al.* 1988: 21). Alan Howe (1997: 61) wrote of the difficulties and constraints that beset the assessment of classroom talk:

- the pressure of numbers
- the ephemerality of the medium
- the power that context has over the behaviour, confidence and language use of the participants
- the way in which such behaviour can further alter the context.

In one sense, all we can hope for is a system of assessment that recognises the need to give all pupils a chance to reveal and to develop their spoken language competence, and which therefore gathers evidence over time and over as wide a range of authentic contexts as possible (Howe 1997: 61).

Gathering evidence of progress in speaking and listening, therefore, would seem to depend on creating our own frameworks. In the next part of this chapter we will discuss some of the ways in which we can use National Curriculum and SCAA guidelines to help us to keep a record of individual progress in our classrooms, which will also include the children as active participants in the process.

Recording evidence

The National Curriculum for English details the range of purposes for which talk opportunities should be provided in schools, and the key skills necessary for confident expression and careful listening. It also provides information about the development of pupils' use and appreciation of standard English and other dialects, and their growing fluency with an increasingly enriched vocabulary as they progress through the levels of attainment. In order to collect evidence of speaking and listening you will need to become confident about your own judgement of individual progress and you will almost certainly need to use some form of framework for recording progress. It is helpful to have some ideas of formats for recording in mind when you are planning the curriculum so that assessment for Speaking and Listening is incorporated into a term's work. Some record-keeping formats are included in this chapter. These are intended to help you to organise and structure your observations in order to identify strengths and areas for development. They have been adapted from a range of different sources and can be adjusted to suit the particular needs of your own pupils.

We can create assessment opportunities by planning to listen to children talking in many different contexts, for different purposes and to different audiences over a period of time; in these contexts we also observe the child as a listener. You will need to consider the range of assessment opportunities available and different ways of recording evidence. There are many formal and informal situations in which information about an individual's speaking and listening abilities can be collected and recorded.

Teacher assessment

An initial assessment of children's speaking and listening skills might begin by considering readily observable features of talk. Table 6.1 is adapted from NOP (1991). This could be used on a single occasion or to gather information over a longer period.

The questions included in Table 8.1 could be asked in ways which would elicit a more detailed response. For example question 2, 'Does the child listen carefully?' could be expanded.

TABLE 8.1 What am I looking for in the child's talk?

		Yes	No
1	Does the child initiate and carry on conversations?		
2	Does the child listen carefully?		
3	Can the child's talk be easily understood?		
4	Does the child describe experiences?		
5	Does the child give instructions?		
6	Does the child follow verbal instructions?		
7	Does the child ask questions?		
8	Can the child contribute to a working group?		
9	Does the child 'think aloud'?		
10	Does the child modify talk for different audiences?		

Does the child listen carefully:

■ to a familiar adult?

■ to an unfamiliar adult?

■ to friends?

■ to unfamiliar children?

■ when working in a group?

■ in a whole-class situation?

■ in a whole-school situation?

Each of the other questions could be expanded in a similar way in order to obtain more detailed information, depending on the purpose of the assessment at the time. You will need to think about the aims and purposes of recording and assessment of talk when deciding which method to use. You might like to consider these points:

- What is the aim of the assessment?
- What factual information is required?
- Who will look at or use the information that is collected?
- Will any action be taken as a result?
- In what form is the information required?
- How will this assessment help the child?

Different purposes will require different sorts of assessment. You might, for example, want to do a quick initial overview of your new class, or you might need a more detailed procedure that will enable you to monitor and chart their progress over a period of time, or you may need to carry out a detailed study of an individual child to support an application for a Statement of Special Need in Education.

Table 8.2 provides a way of monitoring classroom talk opportunities over a length of time. The time span chosen should be long enough to provide evidence from a balanced range of different contexts.

Self-assessment

Involving children in the assessment of their own speaking and listening helps them to develop a way of describing their own talk and become aware of the way they interact with other people. It also helps them to take an active part in their own learning as we saw in Chapter 6, where children became aware of themselves as talkers as they learned to work together round the computer.

The role of considering and recording their own talk can be provided by completing a 'talk diary'. This can build up a picture of children's talking and listening activities over a finite length of time in a way that is straightforward for both teacher and child to use and interpret. In the same way that reading records are constantly updated, adding to the content of a talk diary should be simple and frequent. A comprehensive talk diary can fulfil several purposes. It can:

- provide an overview of the range of opportunities for speaking and listening which the child has experienced
- record the child's strengths and weaknesses in speaking and listening
- build up a picture over time of speaking and listening activities
- focus the child's attention on the value of speaking and listening
- provide evidence for informal ongoing assessment
- contribute to planning of activities
- provide a resource for reporting the child's achievements.

Table 8.3 is a talk diary for upper primary pupils and is an example of a diary designed for children at Key Stage 2 to fill in themselves at the end of a week. The teacher can add any

TABLE 8.2 Monitoring classroom talk

Date	Context	Group names	Notes

TABLE 8.3 Talk Diary Key Stage 2

Name: Start date: End date:

This week at school I have joined in by talking in these ways:

	Week 1	Week 2	Week 3	Week 4
discussing				
planning				
storytelling				
presenting work				
explaining				
reading aloud				
describing				
using new words				

This week I have tried to:

	Week 1	Week 2	Week 3	Week 4
listen carefully				
join in discussions				
speak confidently				
ask questions				
learn new words				
understand others				

I spoke and listened to:

	Week 1	Week 2	Week 3	Week 4
people in my class				
other children				
class teacher				
other teachers				
other school staff				
visitors				

TABLE 8.3 Talk Diary Key Stage 2 (continued)

A record of talking and listening: T = 'I talked'; L = 'I listened'

	Week 1	Week 2	Week 3	Week 4
whole-school assembly				
year or class assembly				
whole-class discussion				
group talk with adult				
group chosen by teacher				
friendship group				
other group				
working at the computer				
e-mail or telephone				
working in science				
working in maths				
working in English				
circle time or PSE				
tape or video recording				
drama				

Topics and contexts: What did I talk about? What did I listen to?

Week 1

Week 2

Week 3

Week 4

comments or notes that she feels might contribute more information or encourage a particular aspect of the child's talk. A diary such as this can be used for a week at intervals as a way of sampling children's perceptions of their talk behaviour or it can be used as continuous assessment. It illustrates for the child the range of skills and different contexts that are involved in speaking and listening.

Table 8.4 is a talk diary and is intended for use with younger children. It can be completed independently or with the teacher, but at first it would be useful to complete it with one child, or a small group of children, so that they can begin to consider and value a range of skills that they may not have realised they were using. This list is fairly comprehensive but you might want to adjust it so that you could discuss particular aspects with the whole class to raise their expectations of what we, as teachers, are looking for when we ask them to take part in Speaking and Listening activities. Talking to them fairly regularly about the way they feel about themselves as talkers will also provide further evidence of their developing skills in speaking and listening.

Describing progression

Learning about talk, how to talk, how to listen, and about the languages which we use to talk, is a complex procedure. Progress is made at different rates as different contexts and learning situations occur. The National Curriculum level descriptions identify aspects of speaking and listening which can act as markers to allocate the child to a level. We have adapted the level descriptions to provide a slightly simplified version which might help you to reach a decision about the level reached by a particular child.

Assigning an appropriate level

This assessment is to be undertaken in two stages. To begin with the child and teacher complete Table 8.5 together. This focuses children's attention on details of their attitudes and abilities as speakers and listeners. The interview also allows children to reflect on the criteria by which they are being judged and provides an opportunity for learning about speaking and listening. Some children will be capable of, and will benefit from, interviewing each other and collaborating to complete the interview. Once the interview has been completed, the teacher has data which can be used to circle the 'best fit' statements on Table 8.6 and determine the child's level.

Identifying and monitoring progress

Because speaking and listening are everyday features of classroom life it may be difficult to detect the rather subtle differences that indicate progress. Children whose personalities allow them the confidence to speak more often or more clearly can be assessed more readily than those who are less sure of themselves, which presents something of a paradox, since it is the latter who may require input or direct help in order to make progress. Table 8.7 has been adapted from a more detailed scale of progression drawn up by teachers who wanted record-keeping systems that would supplement National Curriculum level descriptions (Bearne and Elding 1996: 15). This table lists observable features of talk in order to build up a picture of the child's competence in this area, and so monitor progress. The profile that is obtained by using this format can identify significant gaps in competence.

TABLE 8.4 Talk Diary Key Stage 1

This week in school:

	Week 1	Week 2	Week 3	Week 4
I talked to the class				
I listened in class				
I asked a question				
I answered a question				
I learned some new words				
I talked to my friends				
I talked in a work group				
I said 'please' and 'thank you'				

This is what I think about speaking and listening:

	Week 1	Week 2	Week 3	Week 4
I am good at talking				
I listen carefully				
People listen to what I say				
I can tell a story				
I can talk about things that happen to me				
I would rather listen than talk				
I can tell people how to do things				
I speak politely				
I find out things by listening				
I can say why I said something				
I know when to stop talking				
I can tell when words rhyme				
I am a quiet person				
I try to think before I say things				
I remember things I am told				

TABLE 8.5 Talking and Listening: Agreed Assessment Interview

Code: N = never   S = sometimes   U = usually   AA = almost always   A = always

What I can do with talking and listening

	date:	date:	date:	date:
I listen carefully				
I try to listen carefully				
I speak clearly				
I learn and use new words				
I ask questions				
I join in class talk				
I join in group talk				
I talk about problems				
I listen to instructions				
I remember what I've read				
I can explain what I mean				
I take turns in discussions				
I know when words rhyme				
I can describe things				
I know when not to talk				

What I think about talking and listening

I think about who is listening to me when I talk				
I can give reasons for what I say				
I can ask other people for their reasons				
I think about other people's reasons and ideas				
I like reading aloud				
I like telling stories				
I can tell jokes				
I like telling about me				
I enjoy being in a play				
I'd rather listen than talk				
I like to talk to friends				
I enjoy reading aloud				

TABLE 6.6 Summary of National Curriculum Speaking and Listening level descriptions

	Listening	Talk clarity	Vocabulary
Level 1	Listens to others Usually responds appropriately	Audible	Simple
Level 2	Listens carefully Responds appropriately	Clear	Increasing
Level 3	Listens confidently in more contexts	Confident	More varied
Level 4	Listens carefully in discussions	Confident in more contexts	Developing
Level 5	Can speak and listen in more formal contexts	Clear in a wide range of contexts	Varied vocabulary and expression
Level 6	Adapts to the demands of different situations	Fluent	Shows variety and fluency

	Discussion	Explanation	Further clarification
Level 1	Conveys meaning	Provides some detail	Beginning to extend ideas
Level 2	Shows awareness of others	Includes some relevant detail	Starts to adapt vocabulary and tone to context
Level 3	Shows understanding of main points	Begins to adapt talk to the needs of the listener	Some awareness of Standard English. Can explain and communicate ideas
Level 4	Asks questions and responds to the views of others	Talk is adapted to the purpose	Some use of Standard English. Develops ideas thoughtfully and conveys opinions clearly
Level 5	Pays close attention, asks questions, and takes account of others	Engages the interest of the listener by inclusion of detail	Beginning to use Standard English appropriately. Responsive to ideas
Level 6	Takes an active part, shows understanding and sensitivity	Increasingly interesting through variety of expression	Usually fluent in Standard English in formal situations. Increasingly confident

TABLE 8.7 Observable features of talk

	date	date	date
Beginning Speaker and Listener who can:			
Working towards Level 1 — communicate			
understand simple verbal instructions			
answer questions			
join in with a group			
Improving Speaker and Listener who can:			
Levels 1 to 2 — tell a story from pictures			
talk about the contents of books			
convey a simple message			
ask clearly for things			
talk with friends			
ask relevant questions			
Competent Speaker and Listener who can:			
Level 3 — tell a story they have made up			
join in class and group discussion			
convey a verbal reply to a message			
recall and recount personal experiences			
notice words that rhyme			
explain the work they are doing			
discuss familiar issues			
Experienced Speaker and Listener who can:			
Levels 4 to 5 — explain ideas and stories in sequence			
make up questions			
recall events for an audience			
consider listeners when talking			
listen to and reflect on the views of others			
be prepared to take turns in talk			
ask critical questions in discussions			
Fluent Speaker and Listener who can:			
Level 6 — explain ideas and stories in sequence			
understand complex verbal instructions			
give opinions based on reasons			
discuss a variety of topics			
show verbal confidence in many contexts			
initiate and sustain conversation			

Links with the English Curriculum and the National Literacy Strategy

Opportunities for assessing Speaking and Listening occur in a range of different contexts within the English Curriculum, many of which have been illustrated in earlier chapters. Storytelling, reading aloud, sharing poems, drama activities, listening to tapes and watching videos, collaborative writing and research, reporting and explaining, all provide opportunities for assessment. These contexts allow the child to talk and listen for an increasing range of purposes but need to be included in the overall planning of provision which integrates Reading and Writing in such a way that clear links can be made with Speaking and Listening. SCAA (1997b: 6) stressed the importance of including Speaking and Listening as well as Reading and Writing in the teaching of literacy. The NLS framework (DfEE 1998c) has a more explicit focus on reading and writing, but it also raises the issue of the importance of speaking and listening.

Optional assessment of Speaking and Listening at Year 4

National assessment at Key Stage 2 has been problematic. In response to teachers' concerns, optional assessment units have been trialled and are available from QCA for schools to use at about half-way through Key Stage 2. These are intended to complement and support existing assessment procedures being used by schools. The Assessment Units for English, Maths and Science have been designed to support schools in planning for the second half of Key Stage 2 but may also be used for curriculum development purposes. Unlike the Key Stage 2 Statutory Assessment which is, by definition, summative assessment and monitored externally, these Assessment Units offer teachers an opportunity to produce evidence of children's attainment that can be used to complement existing assessment procedures. It is proposed that evidence of children's achievement at this stage will be used to inform planning and target setting.

Unlike the Key Stage 2 Statutory Assessment, these assessment units include Speaking and Listening, taking into account the fact that the Programmes of Study for English emphasise the use of effective spoken language. The assessment units for Speaking and Listening at Year 4 focus on:

- using standard English where appropriate;
- adaptation of style for meaning and effect;
- listening with understanding, responding to others' ideas;
- participation in discussion, taking turns and making a range of relevant contributions (QCA 1997).

The units of work for Speaking and Listening provide opportunities for teachers to gather information on these aspects and use it to supplement their own assessment. Two units of work support the teaching, learning and assessment of Speaking and Listening. These are demanding, whole-class activities; the first requiring the teacher to set up a role play in which the children discuss a proposal to exclude traffic from a town centre; the second to work in small groups to prepare a short taped tour guide of their school. The children will be involved in the assessment process, using a series of Talk Logs which include both group and self-assessment questions. For example:

■ How well did people in your group explain their ideas/give reasons/listen to each other? How well did you keep in your role?

■ Shade in the bubbles to show what you think you did well at. (The 'bubbles' are speech balloons enclosing statements such as: listening to others/working in a pair/explaining ideas/leading a group/asking questions/taking turns/helping others/presenting ideas in a large group/helping the group do well) (QCA/97/021).

The second activity involves preparing a tape-recording, completing a planning sheet and an evaluation of a guide prepared by another group, commenting on the following points: easy to follow directions/helpful for a new pupil/clear speaker/sounds welcoming/interesting details/lively presentation (QCA/97/022).

The aim of the first unit is to provide an activity that will develop children's ability to express an informed point of view, in both group and whole-class discussions. Assessment focuses on:

■ collaborative skills, e.g. turn-taking, listening and responding to other people's views, asking and answering questions, supporting the work of the group;

■ the ability to argue and support a point of view in discussion;

■ the ability to present opinions clearly and in spoken standard English.

The second unit has a different focus and aims to develop the use of the spoken word to plan and present work and the assessment focuses on:

■ the ability to give clear directions;

■ clarity of delivery;

■ awareness of the needs of the listener.

For the first unit, evidence is provided by the use of teachers' Observation Sheets and children's Talk Logs; for the second unit, evidence is provided by children's taped commentaries, teachers' Observation Sheets and the children's Evaluation Sheets. The units provide detailed criteria to help teachers to make the 'best fit' between the children's work and level descriptions.

This approach to the assessment of specific and very structured activities can provide a model for the assessment of Speaking and Listening in both Key Stages 1 and 2. The success of such activities in Year 4 will depend on pupils' previous experience of working in similar ways and teachers' confidence about planning and organising their classes for Speaking and Listening. The introduction to Year 4 Assessment Unit 2 makes this clear:

> For the activity to be successful, it is important that children are given plenty of opportunity to explore, develop, explain and defend their ideas. It works best if they have already had experience of working in mixed gender and ability groups, and in whole-class discussion. There is an element of

drama to the activity taking on different roles, and teachers should give plenty of encouragement and support as children begin to explore their roles and develop ideas.

(QCA/97/021: 3)

Speaking, Listening, Learning and Assessment

The Teaching Objectives from the QCA/DfES (2003) *Speaking, Listening, Learning* materials can be usefully paired with curriculum objectives. In this way children can be provided with a clear indication of what is expected of them in terms of spoken language, while curriculum subjects provide rich contexts for discussion, storytelling, description, active listening and so on. The following example for Year 3 classes takes twinned learning objectives from *Speaking, Listening, Learning* and the QCA Scheme of Work for Science. Making both sets of objectives explicit to children, coupled with direct teaching of the relevant speaking and listening skills, can raise children's awareness of the value of spoken language for their learning.

Example: Assessing group talk in a science context

A pair of learning objectives can be chosen to suit the nature of the activity, for example:

Year 3 term 2 Group Discussion and Interaction (Learning Objective 31)
QCA Scheme of Work for Science: Unit 3C Characteristics of Materials

Learning Objectives for the lesson:
a) Speaking and Listening: To actively include and respond to all members of the group
b) Science: To sort a range of materials into categories on the basis of observable properties.

Success criteria for these objectives, in child speak, might be:

a) you will be able to explain what you have learned from and with everyone in your group

b) you will describe some properties of materials, and say which materials have which properties.

Children can be asked to work in groups to look at a selection of materials to identify observable (through sight and touch) properties such as hard, soft, flexible, furry, smooth, brittle, rough. Having established a range of properties, they can discuss a variety of materials and assign each material to a category or categories.

During the introduction to the lesson children can be asked to remember that the quality of their discussion is part of their work. If the class has established ground rules for exploratory talk (see Chapter 6) these can be used, with an emphasis on the importance of asking all group members by name for their opinion and the reasons for their ideas.

Assessment can be undertaken by teacher observation of the group; by asking another classmate to undertake a talk tally which records when children ask one another questions or respond to suggestions; or by the group themselves. For example, each child can be provided with different coloured counters. When they are asked a question or when someone responds to their idea, they can place a counter in a pot in the middle of the table. During the plenary work at the end of the session the group can be asked to evaluate their understanding of the science they have undertaken, and the quality of their talk. Another suggestion for the success criteria might be 'We have all had chance to say what we think and our ideas have been respected'. Do the group feel that they have achieved success?

Conclusion

This chapter has described ways in which assessment can be planned in conjunction with curriculum activities. This strategy can help make the value of talk explicit to children. Careful organisation can create suitable conditions for observing, assessing and recording children's competence as speakers and listeners. A process of continuous assessment can be usefully integrated into the children's language experiences.

In early years classrooms, children's curriculum-related learning can be assessed through the medium of spoken language. At this stage, children are beginning to use spoken language as a tool for learning. As they talk about new ideas and new knowledge with others, they increase their vocabulary, extend their talk repertoire, and become increasingly aware of the different demands made by different tasks and contexts. The purpose of assessment is to monitor both the understanding of curriculum knowledge and the ability to express this appropriately. Assessment of speaking and listening recognises spoken language as the child's most valuable tool for learning.

Further reading

Bearne, E. and Elding, S. (1996) 'Speaking and listening. Describing progress', *Primary English Magazine* 2(2), 15–19.

Clarke, S. (2000) *Targeting Assessment in Primary Classrooms*. London: Hodder & Stoughton.

Clarke, S. (2001) *Unlocking Formative Assessment*. London: Hodder & Stoughton.

Howe, A. (1997) *Making Talk Work*. Sheffield: National Association for the Teaching of English (NATE).

Qualifications and Curriculum Authority (QCA)/Department for Education and Skills (DfES) (2003) *Speaking, Listening, Learning: working with children in Key Stages 1 and 2*. London: HMSO.

Epilogue

Listening to children

Three six-year-old girls look at photographs:

23. Let me have a look at this one
24. It's dark
25. The wind . . .
26. Very dark
27. The sea's . . .
28. The sea's all wavy
29. Yeah
30. Wavy and . . .
31. Dull, dull
32. Yeah, it's really dull
33. Dark, very muddy . . .
34. Cold, dark, wet.

. . . .

85. I know, the waves are coming up onto the ground, the land, aren't they?
86. Wavy
87. The waves are coming up onto the ground
88. Yeah
89. It's muddy, very muddy
90. Yeah, muddy
91. That's the sea
92. Yeah
93. Floody, tuddy, puddy
94. Puddles
95. Yeah, lots of puddles

These young children are playing with language and sound, producing a polyphonic counterpoint of repetition that is close to poetry.

96. The moon isn't there

97. It's dark and cold

98. Look at that light

99. That light's fallen off

100. Dropping, dropping

101. 'Cos the wet drops off the trees

102. The rocks are falling into the sea

103. Where?

104. Look that one's sinking

105. The wind's blowing very hard

106. Yeah

107. Twisting, twisting . . .

108. The waves are twisting around

109. Yeah

110. The leaves are twisting 'cos the wind, they go round and round

A group of trainees in the fourth year of a Primary BEd degree course were required to set a task which would involve children in collaborative talk. They could do this in any curriculum area but were to transcribe an extract that provided evidence of the children working together. Rosemary's class was engaged in a geography topic on weather; she wanted to give them an activity that would encourage group discussion and collaboration while developing geographical knowledge and understanding. The children were aged six in a Reception/Year 1/Year 2 class of 25 in a rural lower school. The three girls above were recorded as they looked at photographs of windy weather. They were talking so excitedly that Rosemary was not always able to identify the speakers but she was able to identify the way that their talk was developing. At first, they used a listing type of discussion, a pattern of statement and response (Phillips 1988) which in this case was descriptive. This demonstrated their knowledge of the conventions of turn-taking. As they continued, they became more hesitant and thoughtful. Looking at lines 27 to 34, Rosemary felt that their repetition of words permitted continuity and development of the discussion. As they progressed, she noticed a marked change in the style of the talk. One child digressed from the main focus of the photographs and initiated a period of sustained collaborative talk. Rosemary commented on the extract, to show how this happened:

51. A: Butterflies are not around, flowers are growing, flowers are growing
    (*Said with certainty – this initiates the topic*)

52. B: No they're not
    (*The first sign of disagreement*)

53. B: Flowers are dying, getting old and . . .
    (*Now hesitant and uncertain*)

54. B: No, they're not . . .
    (*Attempts to raise her status as the authority and take control*)

55. C: They're not dying. How can flowers die?
(*C accepts B's position. Her question moves the talk on*)

56. B: Yes they can

57. A: Yeah, not like people die, they don't die the same as people
(*This digression leads to further development*)

58. C: It's really dark
(*This attempt to bring group back 'on task' fails*)

59. A: People could die, because they are really cold and then they die . . .
(*A perseveres with her argument which leads to reasoning*)

60. C: It's raining
(*C tries again with more success*)

61. B: It looks like that pole's fallen over, doesn't it?
(*Her question invites further comment on the task and indicates the end of the sub-topic. She assumes control of the discussion*)

62. Yeah

63. Yeah (*She accepts B's control and gets back 'on task'*)

Rosemary's analysis of this extract shows the development of relationships in the group.

A proposes new ideas questioningly and looks for reassurance or confirmation. B takes on the mantle of authority: C has little involvement but attempts to keep the group on task. In this section of the discussion, A demonstrates further progress in her attempts to used reasoned argument as she adopts a position that is more questioning and investigatory.

Rosemary looks at the transcript as a whole and identifies steady progress from the early stage of listing descriptive observations to this more collaborative, exploratory talk.

Initially their talk focuses solely on the visual effects of the wind:
Look, trees have fallen down/And that sign's fallen off/Buildings are falling down/Trees are waving round. This soon develops, becoming more descriptive and using language appropriate for describing the weather:

15. It's wet, miserable
16. Foggy
32. Yeah, it's really dull
34. Cold, dark, wet

Their talk demonstrates their knowledge of the need for appropriate clothing to suit the climatic conditions. We can see from the following comments that they are applying their own experiences to the situation captured in the photograph:

70. He's got his coat on
71. And he's got his warm cagoule

81. He's got his warm joggers on and his boots
82. Yeah, he's got his boots on, his wet boots

128. He hasn't got any gloves on
129. Well his hands can't be cold, can they?

Using this carefully documented evidence, Rosemary was able to make some tentative observations about what this group was learning. She was able to assess the children in two ways; first looking at their use of spoken language and then at the knowledge and understanding that was evident through their talk.

It was evident from an assessment of their talk, as recorded in the transcript, that the group was functioning in the following ways. They:

- had confidence in their talking and listening;
- listened to each other;
- were listened to and understood by the others;
- used language appropriately in order to convey meaning;
- related their own experiences to a new context;
- spoke with clarity.

These factors would suggest that as a group the children are 'gaining experience as speaker/listener' (Bearne and Elding 1996) and that using National Curriculum level descriptors, they would be around Level 1 to 2. Child A demonstrates further skills in her talk – she initiates ideas and is able to formulate a reasoned argument – in doing so she reveals abilities that are almost certainly Level 2.

Assessment through talk shows geographical knowledge and understanding in a number of areas: the visual effects of the wind; directionality; climatic conditions and how these affect physical and human features; and the necessity for appropriate clothing.

Their ability to use appropriate vocabulary to describe physical and human features and to select and use information from the photographs and express their views on the environments shown, indicates that they are, as a group, at Level 2 in their geographical skills and understanding. The evidence would suggest that Child C is probably at Level 1 and progressing to Level 2 (DfE 1995b).

Interestingly, much geographical thinking was taking place throughout the group discussion that was not revealed in their talk. It was only upon reflection when they were reporting their findings back to the class that these became apparent. It would seem that this is not an unusual occurrence, 'their talk often provides surprisingly little information about what learning is taking place – it is "in their heads". But when you ask them to report back, you will get many valuable insights' (NOP 1991: 17). Indeed, when this group reported back, they demonstrated a greater level of geographical language, using a range of terminology to describe the wind. They also remarked on evidence of the strength of the wind and gave reasons for their statements. In addition they also made reasoned attempts to place the photograph within a global perspective.

Rosemary concluded that this assessment had suggested ways in which she might provide future opportunities for group work of this kind: 'This will mean working in pairs or small groups, initially, to develop thoughts, ideas and language and then sharing their findings, possibly in a whole-class setting or through the use of other group strategies, such as "jigsawing".' She felt that talk needed to be planned for, supported and encouraged across the curriculum as part of a whole-school approach, since:

> In adult life and in the world of work talk is far more important than reading or writing…If schools neglect talk they will not only deny young people a vital means of learning but they will be failing to equip them for life.
>
> (Jones 1988: 29)

Returning to Rosemary's transcript, it is interesting to observe how this group, with little previous experience of working in this way, was able to draw to a satisfactory conclusion:

113. The animals are hibernating
114. Yeah
115. I thought that was . . .
116. The letter box has fallen down
117. That's not a letter box
118. There's no summer birds
119. Yeah, there's no birds
120. Because there isn't, because they're all nesting
121. With their pillows
122. They haven't got pillows
123. With their hay
124. No, with their grass
125. They're laying in their . . . and, and finding new nests
126. Yeah
127. And it's not sunny
128. He hasn't got any gloves on
129. Well his hands can't be cold, can they?
130. He's got his coat zipped up
131. Rabbits are going in their holes, cats are going inside
132. Yeah
133. Ducks, what are they doing?
134. Um . . .
135. They're going into the farmyard and hibernating and . . .
136. Ducks don't hibernate!
137. And elephants, they are lying down and . . .
138. Goats, they are hibernating. All the animals
139. Hedgehogs are rolling up in balls
140. The foxes are hibernating (*Giggles*)
141. I think we have said enough now
142. No, no one is going outside. They're all staying in their houses 'cos it's so windy

Lynda, who was also working with very young children, was concerned that National Curriculum requirements suggest a shift in emphasis from informal talk to more formal speaking, a performance mode that does not share some of the features that characterise the kind of talk that occurs in collaborative learning situations, 'short turns, unfinished sentences, interruptions and occasional uses of anecdote to make a point'. Teachers need to be aware of these differences when they are assessing children's talk. In her analysis of a transcript of three five-year-olds' collaborative talk, Lynda was looking for evidence of learning, of how they were using language to communicate, receive meaning and make sense of the task she had set. She wanted the group, two girls and a boy, to develop a narrative together – a more ambitious project than those described by the students in Chapter 3. Taking their age and lack of experience into consideration, she hoped to do this through role play.

> I chose role play because it can make a valuable contribution towards developing children's confidence in speaking and listening and narrative because it is a powerful device for making sense of experience as children will bring what they know and what they are learning about life and living to these situations.
>
> (Graham and Kelly 2000: 79)

She started them off by asking them to close their eyes and imagine a beautiful shop full of toys including a rag doll with big eyes.

A: I can see it (*excitedly*) I can see her with a hat

G: I can see her with beautiful eyes . . . like my shoes

S: I can see short hair on her

A: She's got lipstick on her mouth. She's got bracelets on her hands and she's got blusher on her face and she's got fing . . . finger things

G: She's got nail varnish

A: Yes (*nodding approvingly*) nail varnish

In her analysis of the talk that followed, Lynda observed that they moved on from this rather polite turn-taking, simply describing things, to collaborative decision making. At first, as ideas were formed in quick succession, the children wanted to express them immediately and turn-taking was controlled by interrupting others, 'I want to talk', but as the role play developed they seemed to be swept along by the story they were jointly creating with help from Lynda who took part in role as a broken toy:

Teacher: The toy mender is not mending us...what are we going to do about it?

G: Nobody will be able to buy us and no one will think you are pretty and they would say 'that doll is not very nice, so I am not going to buy that one. I'm going to buy the pretty one'. That is me

S: Why don't we get the...hammers and tools...go get tools...hammers and fix us?

G: Oh yes

A: Why don't we walk out and get some more tools and spoons and take all our stuffing out with a spoon?

G: If you don't have anything to mend, then you should go to the next shop and buy some tools

S: He's left some tools here, a hammer and screws and screwdrivers

A: Mend legs with screws, put a nail in legs and scoop out the stuff, make another toy like us and we just put a button in it so it says our voices and then we can run out and buy some things

G: And then we could buy a book and look through the book until we find a mending piece then we just walk in the door and look out with our big eyes and say (*she stands up with arms outstretched*) 'Magical glue, magical magical glue, magical, magical, come to us magical we need some hammers and stuff for mending the head toy'

S: I've got a broken arm

G: So have I

S: Why don't we go to hospital...?

G: We could get some new shoes for me

A: Why don't we go to the shop and buy... get some... some things, new shoes and tools?

In a close analysis of the transcript of the whole episode, Lynda notes the children's different strengths. Referring to this extract, she suggests that:

S, although a more reluctant speaker initiates a lot of well thought-out ideas: 'hammers and tools' and includes the others in the suggestion, 'Why don't we...?' This suggestion receives instant approval from G, who recognises its validity and exclaims 'Oh yes!'. S's idea is taken up and expanded by A who repeats S's initial response, 'Why don't we... walk out and get some more tools and spoons...?' This shows how she listens and assimilates information and uses this as the basis to tentatively move the discussion on, suggesting how to use the tools.

Lynda demonstrates how they build on previous knowledge and experience to make sense of the task:

Most of the ideas come from their everyday life experience, 'I've got a broken arm', 'Why don't we go to hospital?' However, when G elaborately describes an imaginative option as opposed to a practical solution to the dilemma... this suggestion is unchallenged and ignored, possibly it is not understood. G's talk characteristically shows little concern for the audience. A reshapes her ideas when they are not taken up by the others, 'tools and spoons' and reformulates them in a way that extends what others have suggested and makes them more acceptable, 'Mend legs with screws, put a nail in legs and scoop out the stuff', supports S's 'a hammer and screws and screwdrivers'. She adds nails to the group's collection of appropriate tools. In the final line of this extract she uses diplomacy; she is a cohesive force within the group and reveals a sophisticated level of thinking and reasoning.

Lynda's careful analysis of the children's talk allowed her to make an assessment of each child's progress:

A pattern of the way these children use talk and learn through talk emerges. S speaks very little, but what he does say is critical to the development of the task. His talk is littered with false starts and repetitions, which may suggest that he is holding his place while he is thinking (Maclure *et al.* 1988: 81). His thinking is practical and specific and shows evidence of an emerging problem-solving ability, but he neither supports nor challenges the others' viewpoints nor makes any reference to their proposals. A has a cohesive role in the group. She is able to evaluate S's contribution and support his ideas while forming her own. She listens intently and matches what she hears to what has been said previously and this informs what she says next. She obviously learns through listening and reflection although she only tentatively expresses her own ideas and may retract statements quickly if they are not immediately approved by the others, suggesting that she has a problem sustaining a point of view in discussion. G shows some imaginative creative thinking although this does not always follow a logical progression or the previous speaker's line of argument, as she does not always listen to the others. She seems to take the leading role because she has the strongest desire to make the discussion her own.

All the children show evidence of thinking which includes examples of hypothesising, predicting, exploring and evaluating ideas. Their understanding of the problem is evident through their talk which reflects and draws upon previous experience. Understanding seems to come about by matching abstract ideas with real scenarios; repetition helps them to shape ideas. Through their talk, which has explored imagined possibilities, the children will have become more adept at communication and collaborative decision making, relevant not only to the drama session or to English but to all subjects.

At present, Speaking and Listening at Key Stages 1 and 2 is addressed entirely through teacher assessment. Rosemary and Lynda's systematic assessment of the children they were teaching shows how listening to children talking can 'give a more complete picture of children's attainment as language users' (NOP 1991: 61). Their meticulous analyses of what, at first, appeared to be rather random and daunting examples of small group interaction between very young children show the value of listening very carefully to what they are saying. They had learned a lot about the children's capabilities. However, we are not suggesting that assessment of talk should or could involve this kind of detailed analysis. It is a very time-consuming activity indeed. But being a fly on the wall and jotting down things that you overhear, observing and listening, allowing children to record and listen critically to themselves so that they begin to recognise their own strengths and the strategies that they are using, is possible and helpful as we have suggested in Chapters 6 and 8. Nor do we want to give the impression that small group talk is easy for the participants. Chapter 6 discusses some of the problems and suggests solutions.

Many of you will meet situations in school similar to those described by the students who were setting out to tackle this assignment. They had been asked 'What kind of evidence of learning can be drawn from an analysis of a transcript of children's collaborative talk?' They often found that children were not used to working collaboratively; they needed structured help. Vyv was prepared to intervene when she felt that a Year 6 group who were working on their own could go further. They were using a set of questions (Chambers 1992) to talk about a novel; one question asked them to consider whether there were any 'hidden messages' in the text:

E: Morals, does it mean?

C: You think it's only a story, but as we said earlier, it could be true . . .

E: Well, I don't suppose it would be an 18 video rating because there's no bad language. But maybe, young children might think it'd be a good idea to run away

C: . . . and think oh good, let's run away . . .

E: . . . and play with matches

(Vyv, who has not been part of the discussion up to this point, senses that they need help with the question)

Vyv: OK, but what kind of messages, if any, do you think Ruth Thomas would like you to come away from the story with?

In her assignment, Vyv comments, 'For the first time, the discussion is marked by a silence of uncertainty and thought. All three group members look searchingly at each other'.

C: *(suddenly)* Oh, maybe they're saying, 'Don't do it'

S: Well, it could be that

And the discussion continues. Vyv, reflecting on the talk that she has transcribed and analysed, writes in her conclusion:

> In the final analysis, it seems that talk as a medium through which to learn, is unique in the contribution it makes. Once basic talking skills and conventions are acquired, a wealth of collaborative learning can take place. Through exploratory talk, by sharing the entire group's skills, knowledge and understanding, the resulting learning which takes place, is somehow more than the sum of the group's knowledge. Learning is taken into another dimension, in which all members benefit from an enriched learning experience. By combining thoughts, ideas and insight, the end product, far from being simply the sum of its parts, emerges as a unique, enriching experience for each participant.

So we have ended this book as we began, with the thoughts of student teachers faced with the problems and pleasures of creating a classroom environment for speaking and listening. Each chapter has addressed different ways of responding creatively to all your pupils' needs in what is potentially the most immediate and satisfying aspect of working with children and the medium through which all your teaching will take place.

References

Alexander, R. J. (2000) *Culture and Pedagogy: International Comparisons in Primary Education.* Oxford: Blackwell.

Alexander, R. J. (2003) *Talk for Learning: The First Year.* Northallerton: North Yorkshire County Council.

Alexander, R. J. (2004) *Towards Dialogic Teaching: Rethinking Classroom Talk.* Cambridge: Dialogos UK Ltd.

Barnes, D. (1973) *Language in the Classroom. Educational Studies: A Second Level Course Language and Learning. Block 4.* Milton Keynes: Open University Press.

Barnes, D. (1976) *From Communication to Curriculum.* Harmondsworth: Penguin.

Barnes, D. and Sheeran, S. (1992) 'Oracy and genre: speech styles in the classroom', in Norman, K. (ed.) *Thinking Voices: The Work of the National Oracy Project.* London: Hodder & Stoughton.

Barnes, D., Britton, J. and Rosen, H. (1969) *Language, the Learner and the School.* Harmondsworth: Penguin.

Barrs, M. *et al.* (1988) *The Primary Language Record: Handbook for Teachers.* London: Centre for Language in Primary Education (CLPE).

Baumfield, V. (1996) 'Spiritual development. The power of the story', *Primary English Magazine* **1**(2), 29–31.

Beard, R. (ed.) (1995) *Rhyme, Reading and Writing.* London: Hodder & Stoughton.

Bearne, E. and Elding, S. (1996) 'Speaking and listening. Describing progress', *Primary English Magazine* **2**(2), 13–19.

Brice-Heath, S. (1983) *Ways with Words: Language, Life and Work in Communities and Classrooms.* Cambridge: Cambridge University Press.

Browne, A. (1996) *Developing Language and Literacy 3–8.* London: Paul Chapman Publishing.

Bruce, T. (1997) *Early Childhood Education.* London: Hodder & Stoughton.

Bruner, J. (1986) *Actual Minds, Possible Worlds.* Cambridge, MA.: Harvard University Press.

Bryant, P. E. and Bradley, L. (1985) *Children's Reading Difficulties.* Oxford: Blackwell.

Bunting, R. (2000) *Teaching Language in the Primary Years*, 2nd edn. London: David Fulton Publishers.

Bunyan, P. *et al.* (2000) *Cracking Drama: Progression in Drama within English (5–16).* Sheffield: National Association for the Teaching of English (NATE).

Chambers, A. (1992) *Tell Me: Children, Reading and Talk*. Stroud: The Thimble Press.

Clarke, S. (2000) *Targeting Assessment in Primary Classrooms*. London: Hodder & Stoughton.

Clarke, S. (2001) *Unlocking Formative Assessment*. London: Hodder & Stoughton.

Clay, M. M. (1979) *The Early Detection of Reading Difficulties*, 3rd edn. New Zealand: Heinemann.

Colwell, E. (1991) *Storytelling*. Stroud: The Thimble Press.

Corden, R. (2000) *Literacy and Learning Through Talk: Strategies for the Primary Classroom*. Buckingham: Open University Press.

David, T. (1990) *Under Five – Under Educated?* Milton Keynes: Open University Press.

Dawes, L. and Sams, C. (2004) *Talk Box: Speaking and Listening Activities for Learning at Key Stage 1.* London: David Fulton Publishers.

Dawes, L., Mercer, N. and Wegerif, R. (2000) *Thinking Together: A programme of activities for developing thinking skills at KS2*. Birmingham: Questions Publishing.

Department for Education (DfE) (1995a) *The National Curriculum*. London: HMSO.

Department for Education (DfE) (1995b) *Geography in the National Curriculum*. London: HMSO.

Department for Education and Employment (DfEE) (1998a) *Requirements for Courses of Initial Teacher Training. Circular 4/98*. London: DfEE.

Department for Education and Employment (DfEE) (1998b) *Circular 4/98. Teaching: High Status, High Standards. Requirements for Courses of Initial Teacher Training*. London: DfEE.

Department for Education and Employment (DfEE) (1998c) *The National Literacy Strategy: Framework for Teaching*. London: DfEE.

Department for Education and Employment (DfEE)/Qualifications and Curriculum Authority (QCA) (1999) *The National Curriculum: Handbook for Primary Teachers in England and Wales*. London: DfEE/QCA.

Department for Education and Employment (DfEE)/Qualifications and Curriculum Authority (QCA) (2000) *Curriculum Guidance for the Foundation Stage*. London: DfEE/QCA.

Department for Education and Skills (DfES)/Qualifications and Curriculum Authority (QCA) (2003) *Excellence and Enjoyment: A Strategy for Primary Schools*. London: HMSO

Department of Education and Science (DES) (1975) *A Language for Life* (The Bullock Report). London: HMSO.

Des-Fountain, J. and Howe, A. (1992) 'Pupils working together on understanding', in Norman, K. (ed.) *Thinking Voices: The Work of the National Oracy Project*. London: Hodder & Stoughton.

Dombey, H. (1992) 'Early lessons in reading narrative'. IEDPE Conference Barcelona, Imprime par l'Université Paris-Nord.

Donaldson, M. (1978) *Children's Minds*. London: Fontana.

Dyson, A. H. (1997) *Writing Superheroes: Contemporary Childhood, Popular Culture and Classroom Literacy*. New York: Teachers College Press.

Dyson, A. H. (2003) *The Brothers and Sisters Learn to Write: Popular Literacies in Childhood and School Cultures*. New York. Teachers College Press.

Elmer, C. and Riley, J. (2001) 'P is for Possibly', *The Primary English Magazine* 7(1), 23–5.

English, E., Hargreaves, L. and Hislam, J. (2002) 'Pedagogical dilemmas in the National Literacy Strategy', *Cambridge Journal of Education* **32**(1).

Featherstone, S. (2001) *The Little Book of Prop Boxes for Role Play.* Lutterworth: Featherstone Education Ltd.

Featherstone, S. (2002) *The Little Book of Treasure Baskets.* Lutterworth: Featherstone Education Ltd.

Featherstone, S. and Featherstone, S. (2001) *The Little Book of Role Play.* Lutterworth: Featherstone Education Ltd.

Fox, C. (1993) *At the Very Edge of the Forest: The Influence of Literature on Storytelling by Children.* London: Cassell.

Fox, C. (2003) 'Playing the storyteller: some principles for learning literacy in the early years of schooling', in Hall, N., Larson, J. and Marsh, J. (eds) *Handbook of Early Childhood Literacy.* London: Sage.

Fry, D. (1985) *Children Talk about Books: Seeing Themselves as Readers.* Milton Keynes: Open University Press.

Gee, J. P. (2003) *What Video Games Have to Teach Us About Learning and Literacy.* New York: Palgrave Macmillan.

Goodwin, P. (ed.) (2001) *The Articulate Classroom: Talking and Learning in the Primary School.* London: David Fulton Publishers.

Goswami, U. (1994) 'Phonological skills, analogies, and reading development', *Reading* **28**(2), 32–7.

Goswami, U. and Bryant, P. E. (1990) *Phonological Skills and Learning to Read.* London: Lawrence Erlbaum Associates.

Graham, J. and Kelly, A. (2000) *Reading Under Control: Teaching Reading in the Primary School,* 2nd edn. London: David Fulton Publishers.

Grainger, T. (1997) *Traditional Storytelling in the Primary Classroom.* Leamington Spa: Scholastic.

Grainger, T. and Cremin, M. (2001) *Resourcing Classroom Drama: 5–8.* Sheffield: National Association for the Teaching of English (NATE).

Grainger, T. and Pickard, A. (2004) *Drama: Reading, Writing and Speaking Our Way Forward.* Royston: United Kingdom Literacy Association (UKLA) Publications.

Gregory, E. (1996) *Making Sense of a New World: Learning to Read in a Second Language.* London: Paul Chapman Publishing.

Grugeon, E. (1988) 'Children's oral culture: a transitional experience', in Maclure, M. *et al.* (eds) *Oracy Matters: The Development of Talking and Learning in Education.* Milton Keynes: Open University Press.

Grugeon, E. and Gardner, P. (2000) *The Art of Storytelling for Teachers and Pupils. Using Stories to Develop Literacy in Primary Classrooms.* London: David Fulton Publishers.

Grugeon, E. and Harding, L. (2004) 'Discovering creativity on the playground', in Goodwin, P. (ed.) *Literacy through Creativity.* London: David Fulton Publishers.

Hall, N., Larson, J. and Marsh, J. (eds) (2003) *Handbook of Early Childhood Literacy.* London: Sage.

Harrett, J. (2004) *Tell Me Another...Speaking, Listening and Learning Through Storytelling.* Royston: United Kindom Literacy Association (UKLA) Publications.

Harrison, L. (2002) 'Curriculum Update', *The Primary English Magazine* **7**(5), 5–6.

Harrison, L. (2003) 'Curriculum Update', *The Primary English Magazine* **9**(1), 5–7.

Hollindale, P. (1997) *Signs of Childness in Children's Books*. Stroud: The Thimble Press.

Housego, E. and Burns, C. (1994) 'Are you sitting too comfortably? A critical look at "Circle Time" in primary classrooms', *English in Education* **28**(2), 23–9.

Howe, A. (1997) *Making Talk Work*. Sheffield: National Association for the Teaching of English (NATE).

Howe, A. and Johnson, J. (1992) *Common Bonds: Storytelling in the Classroom*. London: Hodder & Stoughton.

James, F. (1996) *Phonological Awareness: Classroom Strategies*. Cheshire: United Kingdom Reading Association.

Jones, P. (1988) *Lipservice: The Story of Talk in Schools*. Milton Keynes: Open University Press.

Keiner, J. (1992) 'A brief history of the National Oracy Project', in Norman, K. (ed.) *Thinking Voices: The Work of the National Oracy Project*, 247–55. London: Hodder & Stoughton.

Kress, G. (2003) *Literacy in the New Media Age*. London: Routledge.

Lambirth, A. (2003) 'They get enough of that at home: Understanding aversion to popular culture in schools', *READING Literacy and Language* **37**(1), 9–13.

Larson, J. and Peterson, S. M. (2003) 'Talk and discourse in formal learning settings', in Hall. N., Larson, J. and Marsh, J. (eds) *Handbook of Early Childhood Literacy*. London: Sage.

Lewis, M. (2003) *Curiosity Kits*. Reading: National Centre for Language and Literacy (NCLL).

Literacy Task Force (1997) *A Reading Revolution*. London: HMSO.

Mackey, M. (2002) 'Extreme literacies and contemporary readers', *English in Education* **36**(2), 31–9.

Maclure, M., Phillips, T. and Wilkinson, A. (eds) (1988) *Oracy Matters: The Development of Talking and Learning in Education*. Milton Keynes: Open University Press.

Marsh, J. (2003) 'Contemporary models of communicative practice: Shaky foundations in the foundation stage?' *English in Education* **37**(1), 38–46.

Marsh, J. and Millard, E. (2000) *Literacy and Popular Culture: Using children's culture in the classroom*. London: Paul Chapman Publishing.

Marsh, J. and Millard, E. (2003) *Literacy and Popular Culture in the Classroom*. Reading: National Centre for Language and Literacy (NCLL).

Mercer, N. (1995) *The Guided Construction of Knowledge: Talk Amongst Teachers and Learners*. Clevedon: Multilingual Matters.

Mercer, N. (2000) *Words and Minds: How we use language to think together*. London: Routledge.

Mercer, N. (2003) 'The educational value of "dialogic talk' in whole-class dialogue', in QCA *New Perspectives on Spoken English in the Classroom: discussion papers*. London: QCA.

Millard, E. (2003) 'Towards a literacy of fusion: new times, new teaching and learning?' *READING Literacy and Language*, April 2003, 3–8.

Mills, R. and Mills, J. (1993) *Bilingualism in the Primary School: A Handbook for Teachers*. London: Routledge.

Mosley, J. (1993) *Turn Your School Round*. Cambridge: Learning Development Aids (LDA).

Mosley, J. (1996) *Quality Circle Time*. Cambridge: Learning Development Aids (LDA).

Mosley, J. (2000) *More Quality Circle Time*. Cambridge: Learning Development Aids (LDA).

Moyles, J. (ed.) (1994) *The Excellence of Play*. Milton Keynes: Open University Press.

National Literacy Strategy (NLS) (2000a) *Supporting Pupils Learning English as an Additional Language*. London: DfEE.

National Literacy Strategy (NLS) (2000b) *Grammar for Writing*. London: DfEE.

National Literacy Strategy (NLS) (2001) *Developing Early Writing*. London: DfEE.

National Oracy Project (NOP) (1991) 'Assessing Talk in Key Stages 1 and 2', *Occasional Papers in Oracy No. 5*. York: National Curriculum Council (NCC)/NOP.

Norman, K. (ed.) (1992) *Thinking Voices: The Work of the National Oracy Project*. London: Hodder & Stoughton.

Nutbrown, C. (1994) *Threads of Thinking: Young Children Learning and the Role of Early Education*. London: Paul Chapman Publishing.

Office for Standards in Education (OFSTED) (1995) *The OFSTED Handbook: Guidance on the Inspection of Nursery and Primary Schools*. London: HMSO.

Office for Standards in Education (OFSTED) (1999) *An Evaluation of the First Year of the NLS*. London: OFSTED.

Opie, I. and Opie, P. (1959) *The Lore and Language of Schoolchildren*. Oxford: Oxford University Press.

Phillips, T. (1988) 'On a related matter: why successful small group talk depends upon not keeping to the point', in Maclure, M. *et al.* (eds) *Oracy Matters: The Development of Talking and Learning in Education*. Milton Keynes: Open University Press.

Price, S. (2001) 'Ask the children', *Practical Pre-School* **27** (updated June 2001).

Qualifications and Curriculum Authority (QCA) (1997) *Optional Assessment Units during Key Stage 2*. London: QCA.

Qualifications and Curriculum Authority (QCA) (1999) *Teaching Speaking and Listening in Key Stages 1 and 2* (Supplementary document). London: QCA.

Qualifications and Curriculum Authority (QCA) (2000) *A Language in Common: Assessing English as an additional language*. London: QCA.

Qualifications and Curriculum Authority (QCA) (2001) *Working with Gifted and Talented Children: Key Stages 1 and 2 English and Mathematics*. London: QCA.

Qualifications and Curriculum Authority (QCA)/Department for Education and Skills (DfES) (2003) *Speaking, Listening, Learning: working with children in Key Stages 1 and 2*. London: HMSO.

Qualifications and Curriculum Authority (QCA) (2003) *New Perspectives on Spoken English in the Classroom: discussion papers*. London: QCA.

Rosen, B. (1988) *And None of it was Nonsense*. London: Mary Glasgow Publications.

Rosen, H. (1984) *Stories and Meanings*. Sheffield: National Association for the Teaching of English (NATE).

Ruttle, K. (2004) 'What goes on inside my head when I'm writing? A case study of 8–9-year-old boys', *Literacy* **38**(2), 71–7.

School Curriculum and Assessment Authority (SCAA) (1996a) *Teaching English as an Additional Language: A Framework for Policy*. London: SCAA.

School Curriculum and Assessment Authority (SCAA) (1996b) *Speaking and Listening: Key Stages 1 to 3, Levels 1 to 8. Exemplification of Standards*. London: SCAA.

School Curriculum and Assessment Authority (SCAA) (1997a) *Looking at Children's Learning: Desirable Outcomes for Children's Learning on Entering Compulsory Education*. London: SCAA.

School Curriculum and Assessment Authority (SCAA) (1997b) *Planning Progression in English at Key Stages 1 and 2*. London: SCAA.

School Curriculum and Assessment Authority (SCAA) (1997c) *Use of Language: A Common Approach*. Hayes: SCAA.

Scrimshaw, P. (1993) *Language, Classrooms and Computers*. London: Routledge.

Shields, M. M. (1978) 'The child as psychologist: construing the social world', in Lock, A. (ed.) *Action, Gesture, Symbol*. London: Academic Press.

Siraj-Blatchford, I. (1994) *The Early Years: Laying the Foundation for Racial Equality*. Stoke-on-Trent: Trentham Books.

Smith, F. *et al.* (1991) *Looking at Language Varieties*. Cambridge: eastLINC.

Smith, F., Hardman, F., Wall, K. and Mroz, M. (2004*)* 'Interactive whole class teaching in the National Literacy and Numeracy Strategies', *British Educational Research Journal* **30**(3), 395–411.

Swann, J. (1992) *Girls, Boys and Language*. London: Blackwell.

Sylvester, J. (1991) *Start with a Story: Supporting Young Children's Exploration of Issues*. Birmingham: Development Education Centre.

Tassoni, P. and Hucker, K. (2000) 'Providing opportunities for language and literacy', in *Planning Play and the Early Years*. Oxford: Heinemann.

Teacher Training Agency (TTA) (2002) *Qualifying to Teach: Professional Standards for Qualified Teacher Status and Requirements for Initial Teacher Training*. London: TTA.

Tizard, B. and Hughes, M. (1984) *Young Children Learning*. London: Fontana.

Wegerif, R. and Dawes, L. (2004) *Thinking and Learning with ICT*. London: Routledge.

Wells, G. (1987) *The Meaning Makers: Children Learning Language and Using Language to Learn*. London: Hodder & Stoughton.

Wells, G. (1992) 'The centrality of talk in education', in Norman, K. (ed.) *Thinking Voices: The Work of the National Oracy Project*. London: Hodder & Stoughton.

Whitehead, M. (2002) *Developing Language and Literacy with Young Children*, 2nd edn. London: Paul Chapman Publishing.

Wilkinson, A. M., Davies, A. and Atkinson, D. (1965) 'Spoken English', in *Educational Review. Occasional Publication No. 2*. Birmingham: University of Birmingham School of Education.

Wilkinson, A., Davies, A. and Berrill, D. (1991) *Spoken English Illuminated*. Milton Keynes: Open University Press.

Woods, P. and Jeffrey, R. (1996) *Teachable Moments: The Art of Teaching in Primary Schools*. Milton Keynes: Open University Press.

Children's Literature

Aardema, V. (1985) *Bimwili and the Zimwi.* London: Macmillan Children's Books.

Agard, J. (1991) *I Din Do Nuttin'.* London: Little Mammoth.

Agard, J. and Nichols, G. (1991) *No Hickory, No Dickory, No Dock.* London: Viking.

Ahlberg, A. (1997) *Burglar Bill.* London: Heinemann.

Baker, J. (1991) *Window.* London: Julia McRae Books.

Baker, J. (2001) *Home in the Sky.* London: Walker Books.

Bennett, J. (ed.) (1987) *Noisy Poems.* Oxford: Oxford University Press.

Berenstein S. and J. (1975) *He Bear, She Bear.* London: Collins.

Blythe, G. and Sheldon, D. (1990) *The Whales' Song.* London: Hutchinson.

Bradman, T. (1998) *Adventure on Skull Island.* London: Puffin.

Browne, A. (1983) *Gorilla.* London: Julia McRae Books.

Burningham, J. (1977) *Come Away from the Water, Shirley.* London: Red Fox.

Burningham, J. (1978) *Would You Rather?* London: Jonathan Cape.

Burningham, J. (1984) *Granpa.* London: Jonathan Cape.

Burningham, J. (1986) *Where's Julius?* London: Jonathan Cape.

Carle, E. (1988) *The Mixed Up Chameleon.* London: Picture Puffin.

Causley, C. (1992) *I Saw a Jolly Hunter* and *My Mother Saw a Dancing Bear.* Collected Poems. London: Macmillan.

Cole, T. and Cressey, J. (1976) *Fourteen Rats and a Rat-catcher.* London: A & C Black.

Dahl, R. (1970) *Fantastic Mr Fox.* Harmondsworth: Penguin Books.

Dahl, R. (1992) *The Vicar of Nibbleswicke.* Harmondsworth: Penguin Books.

Dodd, L. (1983) *Hairy Maclary from Donaldson's Dairy.* Barnstaple: Spindlewood.

Doherty, B. (2003) *Blue John.* London: Puffin Books.

Durant, A. (1996) *Mouse Party.* London: Walker Books.

Fine, A. (1990) *Bill's New Frock.* London: Mammoth.

Foreman, M. (1974) *Dinosaurs and all that Rubbish.* Harmondsworth: Puffin Books.

Gag, W. (1976) *Millions of Cats.* London: Puffin Books.

Haley, G. E. (1972) *A Story, a Story.* London: Methuen.

Hawkins, C. and J. (1989) *Mr Bear's Aeroplane.* London: Orchard.

Hawkins, C. and J. (1990) *Noah Built an Ark One Day.* London: Little Mammoth.

Hester, H. (1983) 'The six blind men and the elephant', in *Stories in the Multilingual Classroom*. London: ILEA.

Hoffman, M. and Binch, C. (1991) *Amazing Grace*. London: Frances Lincoln.

Hunt, R. (1996) *Rockpool Rap*. Oxford Reading Tree Series. Oxford: Oxford University Press.

Hutchins, P. (1968) *Rosie's Walk*. London: Bodley Head.

King-Smith, D. (1989) *George Speaks*. London: Puffin.

Lloyd, E. (1995) *Nini at the Carnival*. London: Red Fox.

Lobel, A. (1971) *The Frog and Toad Stories*. Tadworth: World's Work.

Lobel, A. (1976) *Owl at Home.* Tadworth: World's Work.

McNaughton, C. (2001) *Captain Abdul's Pirate School.* London: Walker Books.

Mahy, M. (1972) *The Man Whose Mother was a Pirate*. London: Dent.

Mahy, M. (1988) *When the King Rides By*. Bookshelf series. Cheltenham: Stanley Thornes.

Mahy, M. (1994) *The Horrendous Hullabaloo*. London: Puffin.

Morpurgo, M. (2000) *The Silver Swan*. London: Doubleday.

Ormerod, J. (1984) *Chicken Licken*. London: Walker Books.

A Packet of Poems (1982) Oxford: Oxford University Press.

Pullman, P. (1996) *The Firework Maker's Daughter.* London: Corgi Children's.

Rosen, M. (1989) *We're Going on a Bear Hunt*. London: Walker Books.

Sansom, C. (1981) 'The Song of the Train' in *Tiny Tim. Verses for Children*. Chosen by Jill Bennett. London: Heinemann.

Sendak, M. (1963) *Where the Wild Things Are*. London: HarperCollins.

Seuss, Dr (1966) *Fox in Socks*. London: Collins and Harvill.

Smarty Pants (Storychest series). Ashton: Scholastic.

Summerfield, G. (1970) *Junior Voices. Book 2*. London: Penguin Books.

Topiwalo the Hatmaker. Harmony Publishers, 14 Silverstone Way, Stanmore, Middx. HA7 4HR.

Tolstoy, A. (1972) *The Great Big Enormous Turnip*. London: Pan Books.

Umansky, K. (1991) *The Fwog Pwince*. London: Puffin.

Wagner, J. (1977) *John Brown, Rose and the Midnight Cat*. Melbourne: Kestrel.

Wells, R. (1976) *Noisy Nora*. London: Collins.

Williams, S. (1996) *Good Zap, Little Grog*. London: Walker Books.

Wilson, B. (1982) *Stanley Bagshaw and the Fourteen Foot Wheel*. London: Picture Puffin.

Yeoman, J. and Blake, Q. (1984) *The Wild Washerwomen*. Harmondsworth: Picture Puffin.

Index